Religion in Public Life

Religion in Public Life: Must Faith Be Privatized?

Roger Trigg

OXFORD
UNIVERSITY PRESS

OXFORD
UNIVERSITY PRESS

Great Clarendon Street, Oxford OX2 6DP

Oxford University Press is a department of the University of Oxford.
It furthers the University's objective of excellence in research, scholarship,
and education by publishing worldwide in

Oxford New York

Auckland Cape Town Dar es Salaam Hong Kong Karachi
Kuala Lumpur Madrid Melbourne Mexico City Nairobi
New Delhi Shanghai Taipei Toronto

With offices in

Argentina Austria Brazil Chile Czech Republic France Greece
Guatemala Hungary Italy Japan Poland Portugal Singapore
South Korea Switzerland Thailand Turkey Ukraine Vietnam

Oxford is a registered trade mark of Oxford University Press
in the UK and in certain other countries

British Library Cataloguing in Publication Data

Data available

Library of Congress Cataloging in Publication Data
Religion in public life : must faith be privatized? / Roger Trigg.
Includes bibliographical references and index.
1. Religion and state.   2. Religion and politics.   3. Religion and culture.   I. Title.
BL65. S8T75 2007
201'.72—dc22   2006036958

Typeset by SPI Publisher Services, Pondicherry, India
Printed in Great Britain
on acid-free paper by
Biddles Ltd., King's Lynn, Norfolk

ISBN 978–0–19–927980–7 (Hbk.)   978–0–19–954367–0 (Pbk.)

1 3 5 7 9 10 8 6 4 2

For Anna and Nicholas

Preface

The inspiration for this book stems from time spent at the Center of Theological Inquiry in Princeton, New Jersey, while I was on study leave from the University of Warwick. The Center provided an ideal background for work and new ideas. I also received much stimulus from discussions at Princeton University, particularly at meetings sponsored by the James Madison Program in American Ideals and Institutions.

As always, I have enormously benefited from the advice and support of my family. I am very grateful to my wife, Julia, my daughter, Dr. Alison Teply, and to my son-in-law, Robert Teply, who have all helped in important ways.

ROGER TRIGG

Contents

Introduction

THE CHALLENGE OF RELATIVISM

WE LIVE in a world where we continually meet different beliefs, whether religious or not, and are in close contact with other countries and cultures. Through significant movements of populations around the world, most nations, particularly in Europe and North America, contain a variety of beliefs and practices. One response to this is simply to celebrate diversity, and to be reluctant to face up to socially divisive questions about the possible truth of beliefs. 'Pluralism' is welcomed. This might mean the mere existence of different beliefs alongside each other, but it can also mean that all beliefs have to be accepted equally, and none has a right to claim pre-eminence. In other words, none can be treated as simply true. Diversity of belief is seen as something to be welcomed.

Pluralism can quickly degenerate into relativism, the view that 'truths' are only true for those who believe them. What is true for one religion is not for another. This may seem obvious in that what one group believes to be true, another may not. Relativism, however, goes further than that. It is in effect saying that the world is, for us, what we think it is. The Christian God exists for Christians, but not for Hindus. There is no sense in asking who is right. There is no objective reality against which such beliefs can be measured. The problem is that even such a statement itself appears to claim truth. Relativism often seems to be saying that it is true that there is no truth, only what we believe.

In a long series of books from *Reason and Commitment* (Cambridge University Press, 1973) to *Morality Matters* (Blackwell, 2005), I have argued against the incoherence, and the pernicious influence, of various forms of relativism. Without truth as an aim, all intellectual endeavour, and all belief, whether in religion, science, morality or elsewhere, becomes pointless. Our first thoughts are as likely to be as good as our last ones. There can be no progress, and no growth of knowledge, since no belief is better or worse than any other.

'Multiculturalism' has been much advocated in recent years. It can mean the welcoming and recognition of different cultures, with their varying practices and beliefs, within Western society. No great philosophical issues are involved, if this is on the level of enjoying the presence of, say, Indian and Chinese restaurants. Frequently, however, the word, like 'pluralism', becomes caught up with relativist notions. No culture, or set of beliefs is then allowed to set itself up as a judge on others. All cultures have to be respected and accepted equally. In other words, we do not live in one common world. A praiseworthy desire to be tolerant is transformed into a refusal to allow that any culture can be mistaken.

Relativism can appear to offer a foundation for toleration and respect, but it cannot demand that we ought to be tolerant, since that is an appeal to a non-relative standard. It simply demands the acceptance of whatever standards people happen to have, and if they are intolerant and prone to the oppression of others, they cannot be criticized. Relativism cannot discriminate between 'good' and 'bad' beliefs. When it comes to religion it is in no better position. Some religions might encourage human sacrifice. They may not be the kind the ardent multiculturalist may have in mind, but from a relativist standpoint there is no ground for thinking such practice is any worse than the sacrificial love demanded by other religions.

Once a society stands back from the standards of a particular religion, and tries to treat all religions fairly, there are problems about whether it can accept the beliefs of all religions as of equal value. The temptation is to say that all that is of no concern to the public sphere. Religion is, it will be held, a private and individual matter, and the State should keep clear of any entanglement with it. Individuals must be left to make up their own minds. Yet some alleged religious practices will be too abhorrent for any civilized society to follow that line consistently. An even deeper concern is the problem why religious liberty matters in the first place, and why toleration should be encouraged. These may be the prejudices of liberal society, but what underpins liberalism itself? Freedom can only matter if relativism is false, and those who repudiate the importance of liberty are wrong.

As a matter of historical fact, the standards of Western society have arisen from a Christian background. For those who have been brought up in societies which have been traditionally Christian, the temptation may sometimes be to espouse the assumptions of their society about individual freedom, and equality, and the importance of toleration, whilst regarding Christianity itself as totally dispensable. The idea may be that such religious belief is a private matter, and has nothing to do with the public standards of a society. Yet the urge to respect different beliefs, and value individual freedom, needs to be nurtured publicly, and if religious views initially produced it, there is a question how long it can survive without their explicit support.

FAITH AND REASON

Christian belief is itself under attack even in countries with a long Christian heritage. 'Faith' is often contrasted with 'reason' so that it appears that science deals with what is objective, and can command agreement, while religion is left with subjective reactions. Individuals can search for a meaning in their personal lives, and that is seen as the province of religion. Truth, on the other hand, is publicly established, and that is said to be the realm of science. Thus science gains a monopoly on reason and truth. It is thought to be able, at least in principle, to explain everything. In those circumstances, religion has no function left on the public stage, and can be simply tolerated as a private source of comfort. While science is regarded as the epitome of rationality, religion is viewed as a private commitment, which can only lead to divisiveness and irrationality if allowed to intrude on public life.

In *Rationality and Religion* I argued for a 'realist' understanding of religion, just as I had done for science in *Rationality and Science*.[1,2] Both are equally concerned with discovering truth about the objective world. Religion is as much a subject for rational discussion as science, and the two should be able to communicate with each other. Yet both relativism, and materialism, in its modern versions, are hostile to public rational discussion about religion. Relativism undermines the idea of a public rationality which allows those who disagree radically still to communicate with each other. Materialism (or 'naturalism', tying reality to the sciences), claims monopoly rights on reason. The result of both philosophical tendencies is to squeeze religion out of the public sphere. Religion cannot be rationally discussed, since it is of its nature private. This chimes in with the desire in the United States to keep Church and State separate. As we shall see, however, what started as a demand for institutional separation has become a view that religion and society do not mix.

Some theologians have seen a promising philosophical ally in so-called 'post-modernism'. As the name suggests, this is a reaction to modernity, of which eighteenth-century materialism was a striking instance. Yet attacking science as the only source of truth is double-edged if it does so by undermining the notion of objective truth. Post-modernism can stress the role of particular perspectives and traditions until it collapses into relativism. Science cannot attack religion, because neither science nor religion are allowed to claim truth. Buying immunity for religion from rational criticism has come at a high cost, and we are back again with the idea of religion being a matter of arbitrary commitment. The only consolation for religion's exclusion from the public stage is that it is difficult to see how there can be any public stage, according to post-modernism. It has attacked the narrow view of rationality, current in the later Enlightenment, by removing any idea of rationality.

We must escape from the splintering of truth under relativism, and the arbitrary pretensions of science to be the whole truth. The public sphere should be a place for rational discussion, and it is all the more necessary in societies where there is disagreement. It is the nature of democracy to foster discussion, not close it down. Some countries, however, operate a conscious policy of keeping religion out of public life. Public reasoning is expected somehow to float free of the ideas which very often shaped the countries concerned. Although this book is written from the point of view of a philosopher, it is not, in a narrow sense, a mere contribution to philosophy. It examines the impact of philosophical positions on current politics and law in a range of countries. It happens to concentrate on Europe, and North America, where Christian influence has been most profound over the centuries. At the same time, no-one can be oblivious to the growing influence of a militant form of Islam in many countries throughout the world.

In *Morality Matters* I defended a view of morality stemming from natural law, stressing the importance of reason even in moral matters.[3] Much public law (or positive law) has been regarded as based on such a natural law. If it has no such basis, but merely depends on some real or imagined agreement, law can seem arbitrary. How far natural law needs a theological grounding can be debated, but the fact that it can be given one suggests that Christian principles are relevant to the most basic discussions in public life about the status of all law. They should be admitted to public debate, and can only be excluded by challenging the basis on which some societies have been built. This is not itself, of course, an argument for their truth, but taking religion in general, and Christianity in particular, out of public life, may not leave everything else as it was. It can result in calling into question the very basis of society. If religion is, for instance, banished from the public stage in the name of equality and respect for all, we are left with the question why people are equal. Opponents of Christianity, such as Nietzsche, have sometimes concluded that they are not.

Introduction

THE 'INTELLIGENT DESIGN' CONTROVERSY

Just how far religion can be excluded from the public sphere is illustrated by the controversy over the teaching of the theory of so-called 'Intelligent Design' (ID) in schools, as an alternative to, or a supplement to, the theory of evolution. The theory suggests that gaps in our knowledge about the production of biological complexity may sometimes actually indicate some supernatural cause. Its opponents have argued that this is creationism under another name. This is a particular issue in the United States, because of the constitutional separation of Church and State. God is not allowed out in public. The mere possibility that divine action is being invoked is enough to be seen by American courts as religious and hence to have no place in schools. Allowing discussion about God might endorse religion in a way that contravenes the Establishment Clause of the Constitution. Religion is for church and home, not for public life, and certainly not a part of the education of impressionable minds. This was the reasoning of a federal judge in 2005 in a widely reported case in a District Court in Pennsylvania. He concluded that intelligent design 'is a religious and not a scientific proposition'.[4] He added that 'not one defense expert was able to explain how the supernatural action suggested by ID could be anything other than an inherently religious proposition.'[5] The judge claims that a 'rigorous attachment to "natural" explanations is an essential attribute to science by definition and by convention'.[6] This 'methodological naturalism' is, he thinks a 'ground rule of science today'.[7] Yet this assertion sits uncomfortably with the idea that modern science was itself built on a belief in the divinely given order present in the universe. Newton's theism was for him fundamental to his science. That might suggest difficulties for a clear division of religious and scientific matters into different compartments.

The judge was taking one side of an argument about the status of science. His conclusion was that religion and science can have nothing to do with one another, with the unspoken corollary that religion cannot be allowed into the world of public reasoning. God's existence is a matter for private faith, not public discussion. Even debate about such a venerable philosophical argument as the Argument from Design for the existence of God can, it seems, have no place in the classroom, even though it originally inspired Darwin himself.

For the judge all that matters is that 'while ID arguments may be true, a proposition on which the court takes no position, ID is not science'.[8] Thus we reach a point where debate even about possible truth is excluded from education, simply because the alleged truth is 'religious'. What the American Declaration of Independence refers to as 'nature's God' has become a subject unfit even for open discussion in the education of the young people of the United States. Even if ID is scientifically untenable, this possibility cannot be rationally examined, since religious controversy has no part in public life.

SECULARIZATION?

Some forty years ago it seemed that the process of 'secularization' was inevitable. It appeared to be an inexorable trend that societies were becoming less influenced by religion, and that their public life would proceed independently of any religious faith. While this has remained broadly true in Western Europe, it is strikingly mistaken about large tracts of the world, where not just Islam, but Christianity too, have an ever more pronounced influence. The theory of secularization was a hangover from Marxist-type beliefs in inevitable historical trends, and circumstances in the contemporary world hardly confirm it. What has been true in particular regions for a number of decades was mistakenly assumed to be an inevitable trend for the whole of humanity.

Religion, in many forms, has a growing influence not just on private belief but on public policy. Countries which try to keep religious controversy off the public stage are simply restraining forces which will eventually burst forth in some way or other. It is much healthier if religion is allowed to play its part in public, rational, debate about matters of common concern. Religious reasoning is a branch of human rationality. It has as much right to be heard as any form of scientific reasoning, and is sometimes in as much need of critical scrutiny. There is a temptation for any country to stand back from 'religion and belief' and to pursue a policy of neutrality to all religion. Yet while giving space for religious freedom, a nation must still provide principles to make us want to respect such freedom. If it implies that no religion can be a source of such principle, it is taking up a substantive position without arguing for it. If, on the other hand, some religion can underpin such beliefs as that in human equality, it deserves to be able to contribute to public debate. It is the aim of this book to examine the whole issue of the public recognition of religion, in the face of constant pressure to make it a characteristic of private life alone.

1

Church and State

TOTALITARIANISM AND PERSECUTION

WHAT IS the role of religious belief in public and political life?
Does it even have one? At one extreme, some may claim a
particular religion is true and should be observed by all. At
the other, some may hold that nothing matters but individual
autonomy. Yet truth and freedom, so far from bring opposed,
may need each other. Certainly the freedom to believe, and to
practise, a religion (or to reject all religions) is one of the most
precious freedoms humans can possess. We only have to look at
recent European history to see the horror of the removal
of liberty, and of religious freedom in particular.

In the struggle for rights in Communist Europe the fight for
religious freedom was among the most prominent. Since 1989,
and the demolition of the Berlin Wall, religion has once again
emerged into public life in Eastern and Central Europe. Before
that, in country after country, the tale was of oppression and
official State atheism. The policy of different governments in
the region was, to a greater or lesser extent, to make life difficult
for any organized religion. In Czechoslovakia, for example, we
are told that 'the persecution of churches and believers was

among the hardest in the entire communist bloc'.[1] One example there was the following:

An important instrument for the atheization of society was the public school system. Teachers literally became 'priests of atheism'. This notion went so far as to disqualify those who preferred to be religious from studying pedagogy.[2]

In Hungary, the Marxist-Leninist party had a leading role.[3] The situation was that 'as this party was based on non-religious, materialistic ideology, believers were reduced to the role of second-class citizens'. Religious freedom was supposedly guaranteed by the Constitution but the reality was 'that open persecution in the 1950s gave way to harassment and administrative discrimination in the later periods of the regime'. In Latvia, under the Soviet occupation, the programme adopted by the Communist Party's eighth Congress, 'sought not just to separate schools and state from church, but also to "release" the masses of the people from religious "prejudices" and church influences'.[4] In Slovenia, 'the Constitution declared atheism the state ideology'.[5] In Russia itself, religious organizations were deprived in 1918 of the rights of a legal entity.[6] Their property was taken over by the State, and they could only use places of worship by 'special order of the local or central state authorities'.

The list could go on, but in all such countries, the State, and the Communist Party, were given pre-eminence. The very idea of limiting the powers of the State for any reason was unknown. Certainly individuals and their beliefs were accorded no respect. Marxist-Leninist ideology set all standards, and was not subservient to any Constitution or any abstract ideal of freedom. There could be no recognition of the authority of

God, since that would be to restrict the role of the State. An obvious motive for persecution of religion, and for teaching only atheism in schools, was that religion pointed to a power and authority which the State could not control. By definition, totalitarian regimes cannot allow any competition for the control of minds. Thus they have to take action against all institutions, such as the Church, which encourage beliefs about the way in which secular power should be limited, and authority exercised.

One reaction to all this would be to welcome the separation of Church and State, insofar as it gives rights to churches and their members to exist and practise their beliefs. What was wrong, it might be alleged, was that the State was not neutral, but aligned with an aggressive atheism. Yet from a religious point of view, the recognition of the private sphere, with a secure place for religion in it, may not address the basic problem of totalitarianism, namely its refusal to see limits to State power. Individuals can gain their religious freedom, and a stress on human rights as 'trumps' can block State control in some areas. Apart, however, from the perennial issue of where these rights come from, many would want to see a more overt recognition by the State of the authority of God, because only this, it seems, may provide a limitation on the powers of human institutions.

This can become entwined with the fact that an identity of a people can be bound up with religion. The relationship of religion, and usually a particular brand of religion, with the State is often a defining feature of particular constitutional arrangements. A State's official attitude to religion may determine its own nature. The 'establishment' of atheism would have been impossible in a democracy, which depended on the fact of individual freedom. Similarly, invoking God in a constitution tells one of the limitations on power that are then recognized by the State. An alignment with a particular religion, or a Church, similarly shows much about the history of a country and the way it perceives its identity.

The problem is that issues about identity and those about individual liberty can exert a contradictory pull. A major issue in Eastern Europe has been that of minorities who, for historical reasons, find themselves in a country professing a religious identity they do not wish to share. Continued strife between Christian and Muslim, or Catholic and Orthodox, bears witness to this. The protagonists may not themselves be religious, but religious labels become part of a wider historical and racial identity. As a result, the quest for religious identity can come to bring the continued existence of a nation in doubt. We shall see this in legal disputes about the status of a breakaway Orthodox Church in Moldova. Those who do not identify with the dominant brand of religion in a place can be seen as traitors to their country. This is particularly so when there is one dominant religion, or Christian denomination, in a country. The desire to protect minorities can become pitted against the desire to forge a cohesive nation, with some set of shared beliefs and practices. The threat of secession can often be real. For similar reasons, new religions, or different brands of Christianity, imported from abroad, can be objects of grave suspicion. Foreign influences can appear as a threat to a historic identity.

The ideology of human rights can be seen as the answer to all this. Individual freedom is then protected within a State, which enforces a rigid separation of itself from all organized religion. This is the American ideal, produced by a specific historical background. The question is whether it can be, or should be, transplanted into alien soil. It takes with it a rather thin set of supporting beliefs (usually concerning the nature of democracy). They can be imposed through the influence of international agencies, but it leaves open the question why a State should break free of its history, distancing itself from the beliefs of many of its citizens.

The history of Communist regimes provides a partial answer. The old adage of 'do as you would be done by' is relevant. Those who have had experience of being second class citizens, or worse, because of their Christian beliefs under Communism, should be reluctant to treat others in the same way. They should not persecute, or discriminate against, those who have different beliefs or no religious beliefs at all. This is to re-iterate a principle of reciprocity. We must allow others the freedom we ourselves would want. We should not use our access to power as an excuse for ignoring freedoms we would still want if we were powerless. Freedom and toleration are indivisible.

There is still a vast step from the position of a totalitarian State persecuting religion and trying to obliterate it, to that of a democratic State. The latter may give special recognition to the role of a particular type of religion, without handicapping others. The issue is whether such special recognition means that those who are not so recognized become 'second class citizens'. It is not so much the act of recognition which is dangerous as any ensuing intolerance, or possible abuse of power, in pursuit of a sectional interest. The risk of that prompts the call for a State's neutrality in religious matters. On the other hand many recall that the lack of recognition of any power beyond that of a State was precisely the mark of a totalitarian government.

STATE SUPPORT AND CONTROL

In Eastern Europe old habits die hard. One commentator points out: 'Deep down a state has a strong interest in protecting religious organisations because these also have contributed to the social rebirth of their country after a totalitarian regime.'[7] The problem is that the bureaucratic apparatus of Communism can still exist, so that there is a tendency to retain central control of religion. This shows itself in the insistence in many countries that churches and religious organizations can be legally registered. The restrictions can be quite onerous, and can become an instrument of political policy. It is also a way of controlling the spread of foreign denominations, 'new' religions, and cults. The main objection is often that these originated abroad, and are a threat to the identity of a particular country.

The Russian Orthodox Patriarch of Moscow and All Russia is quoted, with reference to a 1997 Russian Law on the Freedom of Conscience and Religious Associations, that 'it has given society an opportunity to protect itself from the outrage of pseudo-religions through court and civil action'.[8] The idea of a pseudo-religion is, however, a dangerous one in a legal context. The concept can equivocate between a body of belief which pretends to be a religion when it is not, and a religion which is simply false. In some people's eyes, the latter judgement inevitably leads to the former. There would then be no room for toleration of religions with which one disagrees, because they could not count as genuine instances of religion. However much truth matters, one set of religious beliefs can never be allowed to define religion to suit its own purposes. Restriction on beliefs in that way can involve falling back into the snare of totalitarianism.

The removal of religious persecution can be replaced by the domination of one type of religion. On the other hand, the refusal to recognize any religion as an act of public policy means the removal of religion from the public stage. Individuals may recover their freedom to practise their religion, but from the social point of view the danger is that religion will be kept as silent publicly as in the days of Communism. The conduct of the State can be as indifferent to religion as it ever was. In fact with the collapse of Communism, there is a dangerous ideological and philosophical vacuum. Without an ability to draw on historical roots, which have usually been nourished by religion, there will be little to guide the various countries, or to help to ground any love of liberty.

This is recognized in many places, and State financial support is even given to churches, in a way which would be ruled out constitutionally in the United States. To take Slovakia as an example, which is a visibly religious country, the State has historically financed churches, and continues to provide support to Registered Churches (of a wide range), particularly for paying clergy. One writer comments that 'maintaining the status quo seems especially appropriate in light of the considerably weakened position of the churches as a result of the persecution and severe limitations imposed on them by the former Communist regime'.[9] His view is that 'churches play an irreplaceable role ... by creating and shaping the system of moral values in society'.[10] Because of this, he considers that they deserve the support not just of individual believers but of the State.

Financial support from a State can be double-edged. Unbelievers may well object that their taxes are going to help causes they may not wish to support. More importantly, from the standpoint of the churches, there is always the concern that a measure of control over their own activities has passed to the State. The idea that clergy are employees of the State, and have a special responsibility to their employer may be particularly worrying. Churches have to preserve their independent ability to witness, without being in any way subservient to temporal power. Recognition from a State may be one thing, but too close a financial embrace may only serve to shackle churches to its interests. Even money for the preservation of historic churches could come with conditions attached which cut across the interests of the Church. The agenda of any political organization may never be the same as that of a religious one.

HOW IMPORTANT IS TRADITION?

There is a continuing tug between ideals of individual freedom and issues about the wider good of the community. We have to make collective judgements about the latter and one such judgement is how far a society is to have a religious character. Is religion, because of its nature, to be excluded from the public sphere? Does its admission in some form mean that it in turn excludes other types of belief, or different brands of religion? The idea of a public sphere is linked with an idea of rationality. This use of reason enables people to talk to each other, and come to some agreement without fighting. That in turn assumes a background in which we are willing to respect other people, and treat them with courtesy and dignity.

As Charles Taylor puts it, the public sphere 'is the locus of a discussion potentially engaging everyone...in which society can come to a common mind about important matters'.[11]

It is, he continues, 'a locus in which rational views are elaborated that should guide government'.[12] Yet for Taylor, a distinguishing feature of such a public sphere in the current age is what he terms 'radical secularity'.[13] The idea of society has changed. The so-called public sphere is constituted by those pursuing a common end, and rests on nothing outside our common action. In other words, all that has been said about religion being a bulwark against totalitarianism must be swept aside. Society as a whole is not seen as having any divine origin or anything beyond itself. The notion of secularity used by Taylor is radical precisely because it goes against anything grounding common action. Agreements and actions are all there is. For a secular society, in Taylor's sense, its members can look to nothing outside their common agency.

This line of thinking means that there can be nothing outside collective agreements. Our agreement together will determine the nature of our society. There is nowhere to stand beyond the agreement to judge its validity. Rationality emerges within our common discourse. It is not itself grounded in anything else. The authority of God is therefore ruled out, but so is the idea of tradition surrounding us and guiding our decisions. The significance even of the common law, as holding a society together through time, is ignored. We are not heirs to a tradition, since, on this understanding, the idea of a public sphere enables each generation to start afresh. Their deliberations are the origin of their life together. They are not subject to anything external.

Taylor offers this account as an insight into the nature of contemporary modern society. It makes clear that, in some quarters at least, the idea of public rationality is already highly circumscribed and ideologically slanted. Debates about admitting religion to such a sphere would be pointless, since what it stands for has been excluded by definition. All reasoning takes place in a vacuum without any view of truth, and must lack all direction.

Even the opposition of reason and tradition is illusory. We all need somewhere to stand. The 'view from nowhere' is no view at all. This is true as a philosophical presupposition, but it also has significant practical applications. In the field of education, as a Canadian writer puts it: 'Children must first of all be initiated into a particular home, a particular language, a particular culture, a particular set of beliefs, before they can begin to expand their horizons beyond the present and the particular.'[14] Liberal education is, he thinks, always parasitic on initiation into 'a present and a particular'. You cannot, in other words, be a citizen of the world if you do not know what it is to be a citizen of one country. You cannot respect other people's beliefs, unless you know what it is to have some of your own. In the context of religion, it is difficult to respect religion as such, if one has no religious views of one's own. The idea of reciprocity, which we referred to earlier, can gain no leverage if we ourselves have no beliefs in the first place. The only conclusion could then be that other people's beliefs do not matter.

Any society needs an identity, which it will communicate to its citizens. No-one can be a citizen of a country just by happening to be in it. Common understandings and common loyalties need deeper roots than that. The public sphere therefore may be the locus of collective reasoning, but it cannot be an empty space, devoid of tradition and particular belief. Even Taylor's conception of radical secularity could itself quickly become a conscious tradition. A tolerant society is not one without any constitutive beliefs, since its tolerance may follow from those beliefs. Tolerance should not be confused with indifference. I tolerate what I do not agree with, and may even disapprove of. There is no need to be tolerant if I am only confronted with beliefs that coincide with my own. Indeed it is not intolerant to judge another's beliefs as false. What is intolerant is to imagine that that of itself is a reason to stop them being held.

AN ESTABLISHED CHURCH?

Reference to identity and tradition raises the question of whether any State should be identified with a national Church. The 'establishment' of any Church is expressly prohibited by the Constitution of the United States, but national Churches still exist in varying forms in Western Europe. The idea of such establishment is in fact less clear than may first appear. In Central and Eastern Europe churches have to be registered to be seen as legal entities. Government finance can support clergy. Various arrangements for religious education can be made in State schools, and State finance can support church schools, and even Universities. Clergy may be able to con- duct marriages recognized by the State. The State can provide chaplains in the armed forces and elsewhere. Arrangements differ in different countries, but religion and the law become regularly entangled. This is inevitable if religion is given any public recognition, but all these forms of contact may not add up to an idea of the establishment of a particular religion.

The 'separation of Church and State' is much referred to in this type of context. If churches are public institutions within the State, they can never be regarded as wholly independent of it. They need legal recognition, and the State will find it difficult to ignore their existence if they command the loyalties of significant segments of a population. What many object to is the preference given to one religious body, especially if this involves significant social and financial privileges. It does not matter so much if the citizen body and membership of the Church are virtually co-extensive. The continuing existence of the parish system in England reflects a time when this was in fact the case. When times change, and the privileged Church represents only one segment of a country, more questions are liable to be asked. Philosophical objections to arbitrary privilege, can combine with sheer resentment by members of other denominations, or other religions, at being given less status. The growth of unbelief further fuels the argument, and atheists and others can seize the opportunity to challenge traditional understandings about Church and State.

Part of the problem in a country such as England is that because its understandings are traditional, it is very difficult to disentangle the religious heritage of the country from the rest of its history. The repudiation of one can involve the repudiation of the other. Issues about the position of the Church of England can then become bound up with questions about the identity of the English. Yet the failure of the Established Church to represent significant sections of the population dates back to the middle of the seventeenth century. In particular, the 1662 Act of Uniformity made the use of the Book of Common Prayer, as approved by Parliament, compulsory in all parish churches. As a direct result, many refused to conform, and such 'nonconformists' left the Church to form what became Presbyterian, Congregationalist, and Baptist congregations. The process of division continued in the eighteenth and early nineteenth centuries, when Methodists were gradually forced out of the Church of England, despite the intentions of John and Charles Wesley, both ordained Anglican clergyman. This disunity amongst Christians was then exported throughout the world.

Clearly the Church of England was not comprehensive enough. Many in the seventeenth century, having experienced the divisions of the Civil War, were anxious that the Church should include as many as possible. Such 'latitudinarians' wanted a Church which was as 'broad' as possible. John Locke himself was a loyal Anglican, and looked to an Established Church which could include difference and diversity rather than simply drive out dissenters. He described the position as 'latitudinism', itself a recently coined word, and explicitly associated it with the idea of toleration.[15]

There must always be limits to how tolerant a national Church can afford to be. In the end it has to stand for something, and have a clear identity of its own. It can merely identify itself with the current fashions and preoccupations of the nation, rather than standing apart and providing a prophetic voice. A desire to be 'relevant' to society betrays an unease at getting too separated from social priorities. Yet the very idea that religion can point a country to the authority of God suggests that too great an identification with the wisdom of the age can destroy the very point of Establishment from a religious point of view. The Church of England has, it seems, somehow to express the continuing Christian identity of England, without becoming too identified with the current state of society. The great fear of many Anglicans is that they will become a sect, looking in on itself, rather than a national Church representing and caring for the interests of the nation. Yet the latter is no easy task, especially when the religious pluralism which became evident in the seventeenth century is even more pronounced, with the religions of immigrants mingling with the traditional Christian denominations. In addition there is a strong strain of indifference, and even opposition, to all religion.

The fundamental question is what can justify the continued national recognition of a body which represents only a portion of the people. If we say that the Church of England is somehow the repository of English identity, might that not suggest that those who are not Anglicans are somehow less than English? Much of the problem lies in the fact of Christian disunity. The importance of the Christian tradition of the country is still acknowledged by the great majority of citizens. Yet it cannot be acknowledged in concrete, constitutional form, without some form of recognition of particular institutions, which are themselves not truly representative. In practice, leaders of other Christian churches are routinely included in national ceremonies of the Established Church. The latter can justify its existence by realizing that at times it can represent all Christian voices in the country, and even ensure that other faiths can receive proper, public, recognition.

The alternative to an Established Church in the contemporary world, which is most generally advocated, is the rigid separation of Church and State. Attractive as this may be to some, it is not unproblematic even when it is upheld by the full force of the Constitution of the United States. In England, on the contrary, particularly when the Established Church can cooperate with other faith communities, religion's place in society is protected by the recognition thereby given. An avowedly secular society may be prepared to tolerate religion, but it will also wish to marginalize it. The idea that religion is a private matter is a classic way of being tolerant of religion, but not allowing it any influence in the affairs of the nation.

A House of Lords Select Committee in 2003 commented that 'the constitution of the United Kingdom is rooted in faith—specifically the Christian faith, exemplified by the established status of the Church of England'.[16] They affirm that the United Kingdom 'is not a secular state'. One aspect of this is the law of blasphemy, which gives particular protection to the beliefs and practices of the Church of England. The Committee was investigating whether this law should be abolished, but the Muslim Council of Britain said that simply to do so would mean for other faiths 'negative equalisation'.[17] The Committee said that representation had also been made that 'from a Muslim perspective, it is better for the law to protect at least one religious denomination from blasphemy, the Anglican Church, than no religion at all'. Extending protection would be very different from simply removing ancient privileges. The latter would simply be to remove religion from any central role in society.

The public recognition of religion, even in the specific form of an Established Church, can underpin the rule of law. The latter, impartially administered, is itself a bulwark against the imposition of beliefs and practices on those who reject them. The intolerance and coercion in religious matters still to be found in many countries, follows from the use of law as a political instrument to enforce conformity. The administration of law must always be kept separate from political authority. It is also crucial that the content of law should be sufficiently tolerant to allow divergent beliefs and practices. This, however, need not amount to the separation of Church and State. The law should not be an instrument of oppression, and should treat everyone equally. It can have no favourites, but there is no intrinsic reason why it cannot at the same time be grounded in principles that are grounded in Christian belief about the nature of God and of humans. In its pursuit of justice, fairness, individual freedom, and the equality of all under the law, it has seen itself as doing precisely that.

THE FUTURE OF ESTABLISHMENT

What precisely is meant by the 'Establishment' of a Church? It is far from easy to define. The Church of England, an Episcopal Church, and the Church of Scotland, a Presbyterian one, are each regarded as established Churches, but the role they each play in their respective countries is very different. The Church of Scotland is named as the 'national' Church, and it has a parish system and responsibilities to the whole country. Yet it has always jealously guarded its independence, and allows no government interference in its internal affairs. The deliberations of its General Assembly receive official recognition in that the Sovereign appoints a representative, the Lord High Commissioner, and she sometimes attends in person. Yet even when she does, she is seated above the General Assembly to observe the deliberations. She is not a participant. For a Presbyterian, only Christ can be Lord of the Church, and the idea that the monarch can be 'Supreme Governor', as in the Church of England, with the right to appoint Church dignitaries, is anathema.

Even in Scotland, however, the national status of the Church of Scotland is under challenge. Although the new Scottish Parliament had to meet in the Church's premises until its new Parliament building was completed, it appears to want to treat all faith communities equally. Voices within the Kirk, the Scottish Church, themselves at times advocate the loosening of the historic ties between Church and nation. David Fergusson, for instance, Professor of Divinity at Edinburgh University, points out that 'since the Reformation, the Kirk has been presented as the authentic expression of Scottish national identity'.[18] He adds that 'this is no longer tenable'. The creation of the Parliament has itself given a new institutional focus for Scotland. He argues that 'clinging to establishment is futile: it represents a failure to recognise current cultural trends, especially amongst the younger generation'.[19] That, however, is a sociological comment, based on a society in a state of flux. Fergusson refers to 'the end of Christendom', but that is to acquiesce too easily in one interpretation of a fast changing situation.[20] It is dangerous to depart from centuries of tradition, because of current fashion. He does see the risk that disestablishment may result in the withdrawal of any Christian voice from society, seeing as a danger 'the absence of any contribution to the common good'.[21]

Faced with the pluralism of modern society, Fergusson recognizes that disestablishment in England and in Scotland would pose new problems. As he points out: 'Behind arguments for equality there lurks a new form of establishment, the establishment of the secular, which prohibits the intrusion of religious conviction in public debate.'[22] That indeed could in practice prove more oppressive and coercive than the mild nod towards the history and identity of England and Scotland made by the residual official recognition still enjoyed by their established Churches.

In England, there is a closer relationship between Church and government than has ever been allowed to occur in Scotland. Bishops, for instance, are appointed by the Crown on the advice of the Prime Minister. Some may feel that it is one thing for such appointments to be ratified by the Crown, and quite another for party political considerations to influence the process. Once the Prime Minister's office is involved, this will at least appear to be what happens. Consultations with the Church do take place, and how far there is political influence is difficult to tell, given the secrecy and confidentiality shrouding the process. The government has wanted to keep control, because the twenty-six most senior bishops are by right members of the House of Lords.

Since 1976, doctrinal and liturgical issues have been under the control of the Church's General Synod. As a result, scope for friction between Parliament and Church has lessened. Nevertheless, Parliament still has a direct responsibility for the Church's historic endowments, which go some way to meeting such items as clergy pensions. Financial constraints, however, mean that dioceses and parishes can rely less and less on such support, and must be prepared to pay their own way in the future. The Church receives no direct funding from the State, and certainly none from taxation. This is in contrast to what can happen even in countries without any form of establishment. Even the historic parish churches and cathedrals of England struggle to keep their fabric in good order, and are treated on the same basis as any other historic building looking for grants. Despite its clear status as an Established Church, and forms of official recognition, the Church of England receives few privileges, particularly when it comes to matters of finance. This is one possible complaint about special treatment that has no grounding.

Establishment has often been an obstacle to other Christian denominations who are suspicious of government interference, and afraid of too close an identification with government. As the Church of England looks to closer cooperation, and even union, with other churches, such as the Methodist Church, this may be a problem, and something like the current status of the Church of Scotland may appear more workable. The problem is that the philosophical objection to the idea of Establishment has always been fuelled by Christian disunity. The growth of nonconformity in Wales in the nineteenth century brought about the eventual disestablishment of the Anglican Church in Wales, which until 1920 had been part of the Established Church. Similarly the Church of Ireland was disestablished in 1869, since it was hardly representative of Irish Christianity, with its entrenched Roman Catholicism, and also a strong Presbyterian influence.

The situation is now different. Whatever concerns other Christians may have about the precise connection between Church and State, the idea that religion must be banished to private life introduces a new dimension. The issue is not the privilege of some, but whether it is right to retain a Christian voice in democratic debate. The status of the Church of England means that is not forgotten, even if it is only one voice among many. Robert Audi, the American philosopher, comments that the existence of an established Church 'does not imply that Britain is not a liberal democracy', but he does believe that the ideal of such democracy has not been fully reached.[23] His worry is that any governmental preference for a particular religion creates 'some tendency for greater power to accrue to those identified with the preferred religion'.[24] This has been a danger in the past, and no doubt accounts for disestablishment in Wales and Ireland. Power, in the shape of patronage and wealth, is not, however, now in question. The issue is simply one of recognition for religion, in the sense of public acceptance of the presence of religion in public life, both in its explicit influence on individual beliefs, and on an institutional basis. That is of concern to people of all religions, and a reason why even leaders of non-Christian faith communities in England, such as the Jews, fear the implications of disestablishment.

This brings us back to the question whether a belief in liberty necessarily involves the repudiation of religion in public life. Does the equal status of all under the law mean that long-maintained traditions have to be overturned? Indeed the English law is the product of that tradition. If the roots of a respect for liberty, and for the valuing of toleration, are themselves nourished by the Christian tradition, then banishing that tradition from public influence could destroy the plant. The distrust of Establishment itself has deep roots in American thought, and the American Constitution. When, however, it results in the withdrawal of religion to the margins of society, it becomes, as we shall see later, a controversial matter even in the United States.

2

Reason and Freedom

PUBLIC NEUTRALITY?

INSISTING THAT religion can play a full part on the public stage suggests that religious reasons are similar to other kinds of reasons. Yet some philosophers have tried to draw a distinction between religious and so-called 'secular' reasons, in a way that meshes in with the view that religion is best restricted to the private sphere. It expresses at a philosophical level the idea, already mentioned, of the separation of Church and State, of keeping religious and political institutions apart from each other. It appears to chime with secular ideals. Yet the question of the relationship between different public institutions is a different issue from the idea that religion cannot provide reasons for doing anything in public life. However connected they may be, one is a political problem, and the other philosophical.

One reason for keeping religion in the private sphere, and out of politics, is what is seen as its inherently divisive nature. This is a political reason, and overlooks the fact that many political disputes can be every bit as bitter. There is also a more general view of the nature of democracy. It assumes as a matter of principle that every citizen is entitled to claim the same basic freedom and equality. Does this mean that a government must be neutral between the differing beliefs of its citizens? As the American philosopher, Robert Audi, sees it: 'Governmental preference of the religious as such is intrinsically unequal treatment of the religious and non-religious.'[1] This is a recurring theme for those who challenge any public role for religion.

Neutrality about religion means that a government steps back from endorsement of any particular religion, and even the idea of religion in general. Indeed, a government may well hesitate to acknowledge in any official way some forms of religion, even when it is not actually illegal to hold religious beliefs. Some religious practices, such as the treatment of women by a particular religion, may seem inconsistent with the assumptions of a democratic government. The inexorable tendency is for governments to steer clear of all religious controversy, and avoid being identified with any religion.

This may seem to support individual freedom to choose a particular religion or reject all of them. The cost is the irrelevance of religion to political issues. Any conception of the common good, as seen from a religious standpoint, can be of no concern to the political process. Religion can be furthered by voluntary associations of individuals. The latter can band together, but that is their own private affair, much as if they choose to set up a golf club. This goes against the self-understanding of Christianity, which sees itself as concerned with all facets of human life, both individual and collective. It also appears to contradict the demands of Article 8 of the United Nations Universal Declaration of Human Rights, which are repeated elsewhere, such as in Article 9 of the European Convention on Human Rights.[2] Referring to the right 'to freedom of thought, conscience and religion', it explicitly upholds the freedom of everyone, 'either alone or in community with others, and in public or private, to manifest his religion or belief in teaching, practice, worship and observance'. This appears to acknowledge the public and communal aspects of religion, so that a religion can engage in public teaching. It might follow that a religion should not be restrained from expressing its beliefs on the public stage.

Article 1 of the United Nations Declaration sets the scene by referring to the fact that 'all human beings are born free and equal in dignity and rights'. It continues by saying that they 'are endowed with reason and conscience and should act towards one another in a spirit of brotherhood'. The latter phrase may be an echo of the notion of the fatherhood of God. One could certainly wonder who, or what, endowed humans with reason. The words are, at the least, suggestive of the Judaeo-Christian idea that we are all made in the image of God. For political reasons, the United Nations wanted to leave such issues open, but the assertion of the importance of human rationality is undeniable.

The question is whether fragmenting reason into 'religious' and 'secular', into private life and public life, does not undermine the importance of our common ability to reason. It is too easy to assume that the existence of radical disagreement means that the power of reason breaks down. Unless it can settle disputes, it seems irrelevant. Yet the problem may be a combination of the complexity of the issue, and lack of full information. In such circumstances, individuals in good faith can reach different conclusions, and different traditions can grow up and be passed on. That, however, does not mean that every idea is as good as any other, or that views cannot be rationally assessed. Sincerity, indeed, is no guide to rationality. Some people are irrational, if not downright stupid, or too given to wishful thinking. That does not mean that religion as such can be dismissed with such accusations, but it may be that reason can discriminate between different forms of religious belief. Just because all religion should not be dismissed as superstitious does not mean that some may not be.

Many want to avoid deciding between religions, or different religious practices. It may seem simpler for politicians to keep clear of the whole subject. Yet the inescapable conclusion must be that if all religions are treated alike, and 'religion' as such is to be treated as one, undifferentiated category, it is being tacitly assumed that they are all equally silly, and beyond the scope of reason. It is a bit like the adage that if everybody is somebody, nobody is anybody. If there are no restrictions on what can count as properly religious, and therefore a belief worthy of respect and protection, inevitably no religious belief can be given much attention in the public sphere.

SECULAR REASONS

A secular reason might be defined as one that does not build in any religious assumptions. Some religious people might even encourage the idea that religion and reason do not mix, by stressing the worldly nature of reason, as compared with religious faith. Yet faith itself cannot be characterized unless we know what it is faith in. This immediately demands the use of reason. Believing in 'God' means that we have to be able to explain rationally what is meant by 'God', and what the implications of the belief are. Robert Audi, however, argues that reason on the public stage must be of a secular nature.[3] He is concerned about the legal coercion of some citizens by others, acting for religious reasons all do not share. Liberal democracy has to be committed, Audi says, to 'the freedom of citizens and to their basic political equality'. Yet if it is to be neutral about religion, it cannot be neutral about the importance of these objectives nor about the possibility of justifying them. Where are such ideals derived from? What is it about human beings which makes it true that they are free and equal? Christianity has been a powerful force behind these principles. The belief in free will as an underpinning of the ideal of political liberty, coupled with a belief in the equality of each individual in the sight of God, has clearly been relevant. The fundamental principles of democracy may be able to gain significant support from Christianity. Ignoring it, or even marginalizing it, could weaken the case for democracy.

Equality cannot just be taken for granted. Even the opponents of metaphysics recognize that it needs a metaphysical basis to be acceptable. The Italian philosopher, Gianni Vattimo, points out that 'equality will always be a metaphysical thesis . . . because of its claim to capture a human essence given once and for all'.[4] He is opposed to any idea of an unchanging human nature, and so cannot appeal to the importance of human equality for democracy. He can give no sense to the category of the 'human'. Instead, he refuses to accept any 'peremptory assertion of an ultimacy', and, in the name of post-modern nihilism, considers that equality cannot remain one of the core standards of the political left.[5] Freedom and equality just cannot be separated from questions about their justification, nor can they be applied in a metaphysical, and historical vacuum.

Audi puts forward two principles to support the notion of public neutrality to religion, which depend on ideas about freedom and equality. The problem is that they may well have gained their plausibility in a religious context. Audi's view is that as a matter of democratic principle, we should not coerce others for reasons whose force depends on theological considerations or appeals to religious authority.[6] Yet if he thinks that the State should not be biased in favour of one set of beliefs, the same reasoning would not just make the State unable to back any religious view but also any contentious philosophical view, including those justifying democracy. His argument extends far beyond the limits of religious reasoning. He wants to single religion out in particular, and produces what he terms 'the principle of secular rationale', which holds that one should not advocate or support any public policy to restrict human conduct, 'unless one has, and is willing to offer, adequate secular reason for this advocacy or support'.[7] Thus one could talk of public health or public safety, but not refer to the will of God, or the words of a sacred text. This is because he believes that coercion through law of other citizens can only be justified through secular reasoning, which all can accept. Otherwise we will have a situation in which one group, especially when in a majority, can impose their views on an unwilling minority.

This approach may fit with a view of morality as derived from 'natural law'.[8] Its proponents consider that human reason can arrive at judgements about what is conducive to human flourishing and what is harmful, without resort to theological assumptions. Some may think that God made the world like that, and gave us the faculty of reason to understand what is best. They will see it as no coincidence that human life functions best when we live in ways that accord with what is seen as the will of God. If God cares for us, and wishes what is best, there ought to be no gap between what self-evidently enables us to flourish, and what religion demands. However this may be, a theory of natural law points to the role of a rationality which by definition all can share. This can allow for, and even demand, dialogue and discussion between people of very different religious persuasions. It can even provide common ground between theists and atheists. After all, we all share in the same human nature, whatever nihilists may assert to the contrary, and, as a result have similar needs and interests. We all have the same ability to reason about our situation. There is much to be said for this approach, as a means of reaching agreement about common concerns. Yet there is no hiding from the fact that some of the deepest disagreements, such as those about abortion and euthanasia, can be traced back to religious differences, and the question remains whether they can be mentioned in a debate.

No-one could reasonably resort to an appeal to a theological basis for action, if the principle of secular rationale holds, even when religion provided the real basis for their belief. They would be barred from upholding what they seriously believed to be right unless they could find some other justification. This is liable to engender a society of hypocrites who sheltered behind one pattern of reasoning while really depending on another. Audi's principle is intended to provide a space for rational argument in a liberal democracy in which there are different religions and beliefs. Yet it appears to do so by simply excluding explicit religious influence from the public sphere.

REASONING IN A DEMOCRACY

Rationality should above all be concerned with what is true. For example, it is important in arguments about how society should be organized that we deal with real benefits and harms, and not just people's beliefs about what may be good and bad for us. The bad effects of some courses of action will soon be apparent to everyone whatever their prior metaphysical conceptions. Nevertheless, judgements about truth will often diverge, and it may be difficult to settle differences. The worrying feature about proposals to keep religious reasons out of public argument is that once issues in the debate about abortion, for example, are characterized as being about religion, they have immediately to be excluded from the public arena. Yet the problem is clear enough, and has an inevitable public side to it. Should the law allow all, or some, abortions? If the arguments against are seen as theological in origin, one side of the dispute wins by default. Keeping religion off the public stage must weight the argument about abortion very heavily in favour of a woman's right to choose. Some may welcome that, but nothing has in fact been done to resolve the deep divisions in a society about the issue. Religion may at times be divisive, but a society divided about basic moral issues cannot escape the fact by simply refusing to allow public discussion on such matters, and by not letting one side influence the decision.

It may be healthier to have a reasoned debate which faces up to the source of the disagreements than to marginalize groups in society who will then resent the fact that their voices are not being listened to. Their reaction will often be to exert pressure on the political process in an indirect way by the use of different forms of pressure. The alternative to reason is usually the application of power. Once prohibited from the public use of reason for the presentation of their case, they will turn to the application of whatever power they have at their disposal. In a democratic society, if they are sufficiently numerous, prosperous, and well organized, they can find ways to influence politics, elections, and public appointments. The more that religious voices are silenced in public debate, the more groups such as those on the 'religious right' in the United States will be forced to turn to different forms of pressure and lobbying.

Audi's principle may be flawed at the very point it is supposed to be strong. It stops some, and perhaps many, citizens from explicitly voicing their deepest concerns in public, instead of bringing out the implications of equality in a democratic society. By being prohibited from relying on their religious beliefs in a democratic forum, they are not being treated on equal terms with other citizens. Atheists, it seems, can appeal to their deepest concerns, because they are 'secular'. Religious believers are not allowed to. Why, too, should 'secular' reasons themselves be assumed to be of their nature less controversial?

Whether or not human reason is seen as a God-given gift, its use enables discussion and dialogue. We may be able to resolve difficulties without an immediate recourse to religious authority. Indeed we need reason to recognize the reliability of some alleged authority. Democracy itself depends on the idea of rationality, and the attempt to arrive at agreement. Simple majority rule can never suffice. Rational persuasion must have its place, and reasons must be linked to what people see as true. Yet reasoning must also be persuasive. Referring to God in an argument with atheists is unlikely to be productive. Parties to a dispute have always to try and find common ground, and not just stress what divides them. Audi's 'principle of secular rationale' may go too far but it contains good advice to those trying to achieve agreement on a common course of action, say through legislation. Theological presuppositions may be an important factor in the beliefs of some, and they should not be required to pretend that they are not. They may still be able, however, to point to good reasons of a non-theological nature, which also hold as justification.

An example may be that some may have religious grounds for upholding the institution of marriage, seeing it as a sacred institution. Even so, there are many social consequences following its breakdown as a central institution in society. The fate of children, and the issue of their upbringing, is clearly central. It is no accident that the spread of one-parent families brings new social problems. An increase in the number of people living alone can produce a demand for more housing, and pressure is put on a fast receding countryside. Family breakdown over the generations can lead to increasing isolation for old people, who are cut off from their grandchildren. So one could continue. None of these issues, real or merely apparent, are 'religious' in character, and must be considered by everyone. Those who value the institution of marriage, whatever their reasons for doing so, can quite honestly concentrate on areas in which they can gain greatest public support.

On the public stage, agreement is necessary for there to be any action. Persuasion, and not simply the pursuit of truth, is important. Plato distrusted democracy for that very reason. He saw in ancient Athens that the cleverest orators could use tricks of rhetoric to influence the citizen body when they met together. In the contemporary world, politicians have become similarly adept at presenting the right image or appearance, no matter what the reality. The art of presenting a policy has become more important than the content of the policy. Persuasion can become a form of manipulation. That does not alter the fact that, to get others to agree with me, I have to present them with arguments which appeal to them. If they are soundly based, it does not matter that they are not primarily the ones which convinced me. It may just be a matter of tactics that an argument is moved on to a 'secular' basis, so that views are not dismissed out of hand because of their apparent religious basis. Some, however, may still feel uncomfortable that there is still a religious motivation. They may be suspicious of a hidden agenda, but that accusation can be made against anyone. No-one can escape their deepest beliefs. Atheists are motivated by an atheist agenda. That does not prove that the argument they present in a particular context may not be important, and worth taking seriously.

RELIGIOUS MOTIVATION

Audi wishes to extend his 'principle of secular rationale' to motives, and proposes a 'principle of secular motivation'.[9] According to this, one should abstain from advocating any law or policy unless 'one is sufficiently *motivated* by (normatively) adequate secular reason'.[10] It is a part of civic virtue only to be motivated by secular reasons. Yet the idea that there is some deep mismatch between the pursuit of political equality in a democracy, and religion as a motive force, is curious. The influence of religion may not always be beneficial, but it is undeniable that many social advances have been directly motivated by Christian belief. The campaign for the abolition of slavery in the British Empire at the beginning of the nineteenth century, and the American civil rights movement in the twentieth, were both examples of reforms brought about largely by those who were explicitly inspired by Christian belief in the love of God for all.

Even in those campaigns religious arguments would not always be relevant. A sermon in a racially segregated church might draw on theological argument, whereas a speech to a wide audience might do well to concentrate on more broadly based social concerns. Whatever was said, religious motivation should not invalidate the arguments used, although it may explain the passion and concern with which it was said. Those who suggest that such motivation is out of place in a democracy are not advocating civil good manners. They are removing one of the main engines of social improvement. They are even implying that the pursuit of power and personal advancement is somehow more admirable than a desire to follow one's deepest beliefs in serving humanity. If the point is that there is no guarantee that religious motivation is beneficial, then the argument has moved on to the worth, or even the truth, of religion. One ground for eliminating all religion as a proper motive could itself spring from antagonism to religion as such. That is not itself to discredit the position and it is not Audi's view. Nevertheless it illustrates how rational arguments for a position, and the motives with which they are put forward, are totally separable. Rational discussion must not be allowed to degenerate into *ad hominem* accusations about why someone holds a particular view.

The idea that some forms of reason are inappropriate in a democracy has to be a judgement on the nature of the reasons themselves. It is being suggested that they are not good reasons, because they cannot be connected to issues that are of relevance to everyone. That implies that they have no link with anything of universal significance. The argument would then be about truth. Audi himself is concerned about social coercion on behalf of religious purposes all may not share. That raises the importance of religious liberty. The same argument also applies to the establishment of a so-called 'secular' state, since that may have a coercive influence on the behaviour of religious people. In the end, any democracy has to reach an agreement on what should be done, in such a way that the majority does not exercise a tyranny. The problem is that when a significant segment of a population is prevented from voicing their deepest concerns in public, their own commitment to democracy, and their involvement in its processes, can be undermined. The exercise of democracy entails the ability to argue freely. Constraints on the free exercise of religion are bound in the end to be a threat to basic democratic principle.

Some are explicit about the philosophical assumptions behind their desire to restrict religious reasoning in public. The influential German philosopher and social theorist, Jurgen Habermas, accepts that some public justification of religious conviction can be given. There is a great repository of traditional wisdom in much religion, and he acknowledges that, particularly in the European context, it may seem foolhardy to pay no attention to insights that have long been held to be of value. Even so, he suggests, when it comes to the legislative process at parliamentary level, only 'secular' reasons, put in language accessible to all, should be relied on.[11] There must be an institutional threshold barring religion, Habermas thinks, because of the separation of Church and State. As an empirical observation, this has more applicability in some countries than others. As a normative demand, it is much more problematic.

Why should the institutional sphere act as a filter, blocking out all references to religion? Why should religion be excluded at the level of law-making? Yet again, the demand that all arguments must be generally accessible privileges the non-religious (and anti-religious) over the religious. The answer to these questions in the case of Habermas is that he is operating with particular epistemological assumptions, which he thinks have to be presupposed in the modern era. He talks, for instance, of how modern faith has to take up a position 'within a universe of discourse delimited by secular knowledge and shared with other religions'.[12] Yet this means that issues of truth have been prejudged. He assumes that science sets the standards to which religion must conform, and argues within a framework of 'naturalism', by definition excluding religion. The reference to the plurality of religions similarly assumes that all must be viewed in the same way. A combination of scientific naturalism, together with something akin to religious relativism, surfaces. This enables Habermas to commend religious tolerance, but assume that secular reasons take priority. By upholding the idea of the 'secularization of knowledge', he takes it for granted that human knowledge is self-sufficient, and in no need of any metaphysical, or religious, grounding.[13] He further assumes that religious knowledge can only be useful in so far as it can be 'translated into the language of public, that is of presumptively generally convincing, reasons'. Religion must then conform to a public sphere of discourse, dominated by science, if it is to contribute anything.

RELATIVISM AND DEMOCRACY

From Plato, through the Spanish Inquisition, to Lenin, it has seemed that those who claim to know the truth will impose it on others, if necessary by force. Yet ideals such as toleration and freedom demand the allegiance of everyone in a non-relativist fashion. A pluralist, diverse, society may appear attractive, but we still have to agree on the desirability of such diversity.

Even relativism cannot flourish as a philosophical principle, without some common framework, and shared agreement of how to live together. Agreements to differ rest on some belief about what is non-relatively good.

Relativism also has to answer the question what beliefs are relative to. Are my beliefs just true for me, or for my society? If the latter, how is that defined? What is to count as a religion, if truth is made relative to particular religions? On the other hand, truth could be made to depend on individual believers, so that whatever each counts as a religion is one. More plausibly, a religion could be linked to a social group, which is otherwise identifiable. What is the difference between a religious and non-religious group? The questions mount, and another problem is that once relativism gains a grip, it can be applied at different levels. We can quickly become caught up in 'conceptual relativism', according to which concepts are themselves rooted in a particular way of life, and cannot be applied outside.[14] Thus the very word 'religion' can gain its meaning in a particular context, and carry the wrong meaning beyond that. It is all too easy to take Christianity as the standard and to assume that all religions must be similar. Yet classifying religion in that way may ensure that we merely judge other bodies of belief in accordance with their perceived similarity to Christianity. We just use concepts which we have learned in our own way of life and use them in what could seem an inappropriate way to talk about very different bodies of belief.

The problem with relativizing our understanding and ways of thought in this way is that it must mean a total breakdown of mutual understanding, and of translation or comparison, between different systems of belief. If our ways of thought do not apply outside our way of life, we inevitably erect barriers of understanding between us and others. It may be wrong to think in a simplistic way that all religions will be like the Christian religion, and refer to a Being like the Christian God. It is equally wrong to assume that we live amidst such radical diversity that there can be no points of contact, and no ways of classifying beliefs. Even so, the very use of the word 'religion' can invite charges of ethnocentrism. It will be said that we are expecting other beliefs to conform to those in our own society. The problem is that we are then left with little way of deciding what counts as a religion and what does not. That, unfortunately, is the position that much international and national law finds itself in. Legislators are so anxious to respect diversity and not prejudge the nature of religion that they become bereft of any criteria with which to discriminate between types of belief. There is a tendency to shift from talking about 'religion' to vaguely referring to 'religion and belief'. The reluctance to define religion means that there is no limit on what counts as one, and whatever someone treats as their religion is one. Any belief, mattering to an individual, is to be respected and protected. Sincerity quickly becomes the only relevant test.

This view can degenerate into total incoherence. If anything can count as a religion, the concept has lost its grip. It excludes nothing. A more usual temptation for legislators, facing this abyss, is to allow more usual definitions of religion to hold sway, and to talk of belief in relation to them. A denial of religion will count as a relevant belief, but totally different beliefs may not. Even so, the urge to be tolerant and not impose any preconceptions, can push legislators to the dangers of total vacuity. Yet if, for example, religious liberty is in question, it is of vital importance to know what is to count as religious.

The inclusion of the word 'belief' in legislation opens the floodgates to just about anything. In the Commentary on the Racial and Religious Hatred Bill presented to the United Kingdom Parliament in 2005, there is the common refusal to define religion.[15] Instead, there is a general reference to 'religious belief or lack of belief', admitted to be a broad category. As well as being concerned with recognized religions, we are told that offences are to cover 'hatred against a group of persons defined by reference to a lack of religious belief, such as 'Atheism and Humanism'. The dilemma is that any particular definition may impose inappropriate criteria, begging the question in favour of some types of group. On the other hand, if words can mean anything, they mean nothing. The idea of a 'religious' reason, as opposed to other types of reason, becomes meaningless if religion itself cannot be circumscribed. It becomes impossible to protect religious freedom.

The issue is further illustrated in Guidelines issued by the Organisation for Security and Cooperation in Europe (OSCE), in consultation with the Venice Commission of the Council of Europe. These bodies have a special interest in enforcing human rights in Europe, particularly after the breakdown of Communism, and the ensuing drafting of new constitutions. These Guidelines are intended to help with the review of legislation 'pertaining to religion or belief'. A major issue we are told, is that 'to the extent that legislation included definitions, the text should be reviewed carefully to ensure they are not discriminating and that they do not prejudge some religions or fundamental beliefs at the expense of others'.[16] In this context, we are told, 'beliefs' typically pertain 'to deeply held conscientious beliefs that are fundamental about the human condition and the world'. It is none too clear who decides what is fundamental, although atheism and agnosticism are explicitly mentioned. What the document is anxious to avoid, for example, is to assume that all religion involves belief in God, thus excluding Buddhism, which, it says is not theistic, and Hinduism, which it terms polytheistic. It sees, too, the dangers of dismissing minority religious movements as 'cults' or 'sects'. Some countries are ready to do this, largely because they see them as foreign imports, undermining local identity.

The problem with the encouragement of diversity is how far even religious toleration has to have its limits. We shall look in the next chapter at problems about content, but, for a start, there must be some limits to the classification of religion, and even of 'fundamental belief'. Examples arise particularly when people are trying to exploit the legal toleration of religion for their own advantage. For instance, the Church of the New Song was founded in the early 1970s by an inmate of an American federal jail. It required prisoners to be served Harvey's Bristol Cream sherry and steak every Friday at 5 p.m. This would be laughable but for the fact that the Eighth Circuit of the U.S. Court of Appeals actually concurred with a district court that this was a genuine religion which should be freely exercised.[17]

Relativism appears to encourage toleration by not imposing external, and possibly inappropriate, standards both for classification and for judgement of content. Yet freedom of religion cannot itself be a relative value. We have to be on our guard against those who wish to destroy freedom, and who themselves practice intolerance. Relativism takes its stand on a desire for equal treatment of different beliefs. If, though, this is because of a belief in the importance of human equality and dignity, these are not relative values. The category of the human is of universal importance and religions must be unacceptable when they aim to undermine respect for all humans.

Why should any 'religion' appear to be sacrosanct, even if it is repugnant, evil, or just plain daft? We seem to be presented with a choice between persecution or total acceptance. Once we make distinctions, we are accused of using the standards of one conceptual system to judge another, or appealing to our own idea of truth to coerce others. That may seem a defence of freedom, but it is actually an assault on reason. We have to refrain from assessing religion rationally, to the extent of being afraid to use reason, even to establish what is in the category. Relativism cannot cope with the idea of reason, except within delimited areas, each with their own standards. As a result, it cannot stand back to judge between religions, or have any general criterion as to what is to count as a religion. It takes all so-called 'religions' at face value, and treats them in the same way, without investigating the content of their beliefs. This is to destroy rationality. We must be able to make rational distinctions between religion and other forms of belief, and between different types of religion, Even within the ambit of Christianity, discriminations have to be made. Not everything done in its name will be equally good, according to the standards of Christianity itself.

This refusal to distinguish between different kinds of religious and quasi-religious belief arises because of the banishment of religion from the public sphere. The resources of 'public reason' are kept apart from religion, and the latter is ring-fenced, and protected. It is, however, also marginalized. It cannot contribute to public debates about truth, and issues about truth and rationality are regarded as irrelevant to religion. It is tolerated, but otherwise ignored. If, however, public debate can include religious perspectives, we are engaged in a different exercise. Religions are no longer kept in self-contained compartments. Reasoning about religion is not simply the imposition of the assumptions of one way of life on another. Instead, as inhabitants of one, common world, facing similar problems, we can discuss issues about truth, without making artificial distinctions between religious and other kinds of truth.

Relativism is not the friend of democracy. It solidifies disagreements into divergent strands of belief. Reason, on the other hand, shows a way of dealing with disputes. There is no reason to believe anything in the first place without any distinction between truth and falsity. Truth is not a private matter, but of universal concern, and only freedom can provide the conditions in which debate about it can take place. The assertion of truth is not a threat to freedom, but its precondition. The alternative to free debate is coercion.

We happen to live in societies which for the moment value individual liberty and uphold toleration to those who differ. There is even a celebration of diversity. Yet this is thin support for freedom. Fashions can change. Freedom needs a strong belief that it must be respected by everyone everywhere. That demand needs rational support, since it depends on insights into what is true about humanity and our place in the world. Without truth, there can be no rationality, and no way of distinguishing one body of belief from another. That is not the epitome of tolerance. It is a prescription for allowing the enemies of freedom to advance without any rational discussion about what they are doing.

3

Religious Liberty

LIMITATIONS ON FREEDOM?

FREEDOM OF religion has long been regarded as a corner-stone of a free society. Individuals must be free to choose their own religion, to leave it if they wish, to reject all religion, or just to be indifferent. The alternative is that individuals are not trusted to make up their own minds about what they think matters, and that is the very antithesis of democracy. Yet some practices, such as human sacrifice or cannibalism, should not be tolerated just because they purport to be religious. The very conception of human beings upholding their liberty and equality entails that they should be protected from the ill-treatment of others. If all human beings matter, and should be free, there are ways they should not be treated even in the name of religion. The basis of religious liberty in ideas of human nature suggests that, in the name of human flourishing, it cannot be unrestricted. How far, though, should religious freedom be limited? The European Convention on Human Rights asserts in Article 9 an absolute right to 'freedom of thought, conscience and religion'.[1] Its second clause states:

Freedom to manifest one's religion or beliefs shall be subject only to such limitations as are prescribed by law and are necessary in a democratic society in the interests of public safety, for the protection of public order, health or morals, or for the protection of the rights and freedoms of others.

The Constitution of the United States is less wordy on the subject, and seems to make the free exercise of religion an unqualified right, with the assertion of the Bill of Rights that 'Congress shall make no law respecting an establishment of religion, or prohibiting the free exercise thereof.' The more that 'religion and belief' are undefined, the more there is bound to be a searching test of so-called 'religious' practices. If they can include just about anything, it will be less possible to defend automatically the free exercise of religion. The American stress on 'religion' alone is significant, and the issue of what is to count specifically as religion will be more pressing. Some conveniently wish to pretend that differences between 'religions' do not matter. For example, a Brazilian lawyer, President of the Inter-American Court of Human Rights, says that religions 'disclose a universal common heritage, in emphasizing ethical and spiritual values'.[2]

Adherents of some different religions may agree more than is sometimes recognized, particularly when faced with the secularist and materialist assumptions prevalent in many countries. Nevertheless there will always be examples of genuinely religious practices, following clear differences in belief, which will be difficult to tolerate. These can occur not just in the context of different world religions, but even in the case of different off-shoots from orthodox Christianity. A notorious example was that of the practice of polygamy, particularly in the nineteenth century by members of the Church of Jesus Christ of Latter Day Saints (or Mormons). Called by one writer, 'the most vexed issue of religious liberty in all American history', a series of cases before the U.S. Supreme Court from 1879 ensured that the practice was absolutely prohibited.[3] The Mormons banned it in 1890.

What criteria are to be adopted for limits to be placed on religious practices? One source in a country which is predominantly Christian (as the nineteenth century United States was) would be orthodox Christian belief. We could champion monogamy, saying that anything else would undermine the Christian basis of the society. Yet some would think that that makes nonsense of a belief in religious freedom, so that one is only free to put one's religion into practice, as long as the practices are consistent with the basic tenets of Christianity. Even if a belief in religious freedom is rooted in Christianity, such a limited view of its application might seem hypocritical. Yet a country proud of its Christian heritage, and its nurturing of freedom, might feel reluctant to put the former at risk by indulging the latter.

The nineteenth-century U.S. Supreme Court turned to a distinction between belief and behaviour, with the Chief Justice saying[4] of religious freedom that it 'could be absolute only in matters of belief, not behaviour', but that must make religious freedom a fairly empty affair. There is little point in believing what I like, if I am not allowed to put my beliefs into practice. Totalitarian regimes will find it difficult to reach into the recesses of their citizens' minds, and control what they really believe. They would be able to enforce conformity in practice, and that shows that freedom of belief, without any freedom to practice it, can mean little for those who want liberty for themselves and their families.

Polygamy continues to be a vexed issue. Western societies make it illegal, whilst there are always some religious groups which try to practise it. The basic issue is how far the free exercise of religion demands exemption from the criminal law. If a democratic society has good reasons for banning a practice, and the law is to apply equally to all, opt-out clauses for religions are not only hard to justify, but may lead to the fragmentation of the society. One argument may be that if a provision is made for the good of everyone, such as the banning of human sacrifice, or of polygamy, the fact that it restricts some religions is irrelevant. The law is not particularly aimed at them. It is not intended to prevent the free exercise of religion, even if it happens to have that effect in some cases. Yet practitioners of a minority religion may still feel coerced. A law that makes Sunday a public rest day, without provision for other religions may appear unfair to those who wish to worship on Friday or Saturday, and are prevented because of their work. Granting exemptions in particular cases to special groups can ameliorate the problem. An example was the Road Traffic Act of 1988 in the United Kingdom, which expressly allowed Sikhs to wear turbans instead of the required helmet on motor-cycles.

CHRISTIAN SCIENCE

Disputes may remain, particularly when the religious views of parents appear to harm children. What is contested is precisely the notion of harm which is being applied. Nowhere does this become clearer than in arguments about medical treatment for children. For example, so-called 'Christian Science', an influential body with palatial headquarters in Boston, Massachusetts, 'sees a person as an expression of divine Mind, not matter, and the human body as shaped by the comprehension of each individual'.[5] The material world is seen as a mere projection of mind. As one writer puts it:

For Christian Scientists, 'disease' is misunderstanding: for non-Scientists, disease is physical disorder in an organic physical system. This is the conflict between religious idealism and secular materialism, twain that cannot meet.

In other words, the body on its own cannot be made to function properly, since it has no independent existence. This conclusion is doubtless helped by the assumption that religion has to deny the reality of the physical world. This is in contradiction to the orthodox Christian belief in the Incarnation. Similarly, medical science does not need to be exclusively secular and materialist, but can itself recognize the active role of mind. However that may be, Christian Scientists see a radical distinction between their religious outlook and the search for physical cures for disease. Adults may have freedom to withhold informed consent for medical treatment, but should parents impose the effects of their religious beliefs on their children even if that causes suffering, and even death? Does the law have a duty to protect the young?

One philosopher puts it this way: 'From the legal and medical perspective, the Christian Science community simply cannot be trusted by the dominant community to do what is best for their children, without serious threats to the fundamental rights of those children.'[6] He quotes a case where a child with a bowel obstruction died because his parents were Christian Scientists who did not understand what was wrong, and sought help from a Christian Science practitioner. Yet the problem is also illustrated by another case referred to in which Christian

Science parents refused chemotherapy and radiation for a child, whose recovery was in any case problematic. Even parents who had faith in medical science might wonder if the suffering and side-effects produced by the treatment would be justifiable, in what might be a vain attempt to save life. Indeed the treatment could even hasten death. Anyone might sympathize with such an agonizing choice. Yet that did not prevent some demanding that the law intervene to remove the child from its parents. The Delaware Supreme Court sided with the parents, but the hospital had wanted the child placed with foster parents.

Disputes like this may appear to be about abuse or neglect, but the reality is an argument about what is in the child's best interests. The parents' view of the world, stemming from their religious outlook was at variance with that of the majority of their society. What is the right response of the law when faced with an apparent choice between a child's welfare, and the free exercise of religion? Has it a right, even a duty, to impose the assumptions of the majority on particular parents, to protect children? The problem is whether the state can act as arbiter. What it sees as 'protection', can also appear to be the coercion of those who reject what they see as secular materialism.

The authorities of even a benevolent state can easily see Christian Science, and other minority sects, such as the Jehovah's Witnesses, as inherently irrational. Indeed, it is very easy for the intelligentsia in modern society to see all religion as irrational, and simply give it all equal protection without any distinction. There are continuing problems when the interests of children are involved, and the question of parental rights comes to the fore. The tendency is to retreat from making any distinction between the 'main-stream' and the plain weird. As one legal scholar puts it, concerning the United States:

The assumption that all religions are at root irrational has favoured marginal groups, leading to a special solicitude for idiosyncratic beliefs, that liberal justices, conscious of their own lack of sympathy for such beliefs, are determined to protect.[7]

'Faith' is made radically distinct from 'reason', and that makes distinctions between religions impossible on any rational basis. They then have all to be treated in the same way.

The demands of a cohesive society ensure that absolute neutrality to all possible practices is impossible. No society could survive once anything is allowed, as long as religion is invoked. No legal system can itself exist without being based on substantive beliefs about what is good and bad for humans. Law is blind without some conception of human nature and what allows it to flourish.[8] It cannot know what to allow and what to forbid.

One temptation will be to ignore the content of any belief, and to concentrate on the fact that it is held. The relevant factors become whether it is sincerely held, and how strongly it is held. That could result in the most fanatical being given most legal protection. The idea that religious liberty must be allowed to 'trump' the criminal law is a dangerous one. Much reasoning does not need to retreat to the abstraction of world-views. Those who see a commonality between all religion can be fairly accused of wishful thinking, but issues about human good and harm can often be very clear. Even Christian Scientists will agree with the medical profession about the desirability of eradicating disease. They disagree in their understanding of its nature, and of how to cure it. That gives the basis for a rational debate about how far the state should intervene.

Anyone might agree that decisions about aggressive treatment in desperate cases may be best left to the patient and the family, even when a child is involved. On the other hand, many

Christian Scientists might see the point of accepting medical treatment for something like a bowel obstruction, which could be seen as 'mechanical' in nature. The problem is that in so doing they may be admitting the reality of the physical world, and denying their beliefs. There may still be a clash between the clear interests of the child, and even its right to life, and the particular beliefs of the parents. Classifying the beliefs of the parents as religious does little to decide how good their reasons are. In such a case, the potential for harm is so great that it could hardly be outweighed by an appeal to religious liberty. Freedom to harm children, and to let them die, cannot be safe-guarded.

THE AMISH

The issue of the interests of children was raised in the first exemption from the criminal law made in the United States. It concerned the Amish people, who live in different communities in several American States. Visitors to Lancaster County in Pennsylvania will see that some there live very differently from other contemporary Americans. It is a prime tourist destination for that reason. Small details indicate a way of life that makes little concession to modern technology. Washing flaps from clothes lines outside in the breeze, as it used to elsewhere before washing machines and dryers were in common use. Above all, plainly dressed people ride along the roads with a horse and buggy, as cars rush impatiently by.

The Amish are of Anabaptist origin, and came to North America in the eighteenth century searching for religious freedom. They have survived and flourished as a separate community over nearly three centuries. There is a theological reason for this. They take up Reformation teaching of 'two kingdoms', of the world and of Christ. They went further than Calvin in applying the doctrine, and see the Church as a spiritual society to be kept apart from the kingdom of this world. To the Amish, Christ's statement to Pilate that 'my kingdom is not of this world' implies that the two kingdoms can have nothing in common.[9] The Amish have tried not to be governed by the standards and fashions of society, wishing to keep away from politics and involvement with government. They cooperate as long as that does not cut across their religious conscience, and interfere with the life of their community. They pay taxes but are reluctant to rely on social security, preferring to look to their own community for support.

A desire to be separate, whilst living in the middle of another society, will cause problems. Even the issue of warning signs on their slow moving buggies has caused problems, because the Amish objected to the 'worldly symbolism' of a red and orange triangle on the rear.[10] After a series of court cases, the Minnesota Supreme Court concluded in 1990 that reflective tape, and a lighted red lantern, would suffice at night.[11] When such an apparently trivial issue is contentious, questions about the education of children will be more so. The Amish are suspicious of the outside influences to which their children could be subject in state schools. A central aspect of religious liberty, if it means anything, must be the right to pass on one's religious views to one's children. When religion cannot be transmitted to the next generation, it is not being freely exercised.

The Amish, however, have wanted much more than the right to organize Amish schools. They so want to insulate children from secular influences, that their resistance has grown not just to public education, but to secondary education as such. The raising of the school-leaving age, and the widening of the curriculum, have exacerbated the situation. Legal conflicts have arisen when small country schools have been consolidated, and when Amish parents have been encouraged to send their children to high school. The Kansas Supreme Court is quoted as agreeing with the view that 'compulsory school attendance is not a religious issue'.[12] Eventually, the U.S. Supreme Court ruled unanimously in 1972 that the Amish had a right to refuse to send their children to high school, and did not have to send them to school after the eighth grade.[13] This was a landmark case concerning religious freedom since the Court maintained that compulsory education 'would grossly endanger, if not destroy, the free exercise of Amish religious beliefs'.[14] The particular concern was that the children would be exposed to worldly values, contrary to their religious beliefs.

Similar arguments have resulted in exemption from child labour laws. Amish young people are now allowed to take an apprenticeship, when they leave school at 14. From 2004, any sect in the United States, whose established teachings forbid education after the eighth grade, may put its children into wood workshops, subject to safeguards.[15] These have become a central form of business for the Amish, who are tempted to sell their farms because of soaring land prices. Yet the underlying issue of principle remains. If 'child labour' is regarded as putting children at risk in various ways, not least from machinery and tools, being Amish does not alter that danger. In the same way, education at high school standard is either important or it is not, regardless of religion. There could be a case for Amish secondary schools, but depriving some young people of education must be questionable, if it is thought necessary for other children. If apprenticeships are seen as a satisfactory substitute for school, they should be available for all. Keeping a religion or a sect in a separate legal compartment means in a case like this that the state admits that it does not believe in the importance of universal education.

Conscientious objection to military service has long produced arguments between the Amish and the government. They are not alone in their pacifist principles, and it is accepted practice in many countries to recognize that an objection to war and killing as a result of deeply held beliefs should be a reason for exemption. Normally, however, there would be a demand that such objectors give public service of some other kind to help a war effort. They are not allowed to opt out of their duties as citizens, even if their moral principles in this extreme case are respected.[16] Yet that is just what the Amish wish to do in a variety of cases, such as participation in the state sponsored system of social security, including Medicare.

These may seem to be examples of problems arising in any democracy in which people have to live together, even though their basic beliefs may diverge. Yet the Amish provide a more radical illustration, because they try to live a separate life, unaffected by the influences of the wider community around them. Religious understandings permeate their life, and any clash between Amish practice and the law will always be seen as religious in nature. They pay their taxes, conduct trade, and profit from tourism. They can never be totally unrelated to the world around them, even though their religious beliefs deliberately set them apart, and occasionally put them in direct conflict with the laws of the wider society. Nothing illustrates more starkly the problem of how minorities should be treated, when they challenge the assumptions of the majority. Making them conform is tantamount to tyranny by the majority, and certainly does not respect religious freedom. Letting them act as they wish in accordance with their religion risks the progressive breakdown of society. If each person can opt out of the requirements of law for reasons of conscience, the law will soon be impotent.

The cause of the Amish is no doubt assisted by a general admiration for the perceived simplicity of their life, and by nostalgia for a time when the pace of life was governed by the speed of a horse and trap. Yet tolerating a charming anachronism is different from accepting that religious claims, of whatever kind, can always block the operation of law, even when the welfare of children is in question. Despite the importance of toleration of beliefs that may not be generally held, limits have to be placed on what even a free and democratic society should allow. Suggesting that nothing should be legally restrained, if it is done in the name of religion, is to say that we are all incapable of distinguishing between our own beliefs, and what can be acceptable in a free society. We should be able to reason about what is deeply harmful to individuals and the community, without merely imposing our personal views on others. Otherwise we have to admit that ideas of good and harm are notions which are only relative to particular systems of belief, and have no general validity. The fact that I disagree with something is very far from a reason for banning it. It does not follow that nothing should be banned with which I, or a majority in a society, disagree. The slide from one to the other can only take place under the influence of relativism. One can, though, refer to the harmfulness of the practices of someone else's religion without begging the question. Murder is murder even if it has a religious significance in a ritual sacrifice. Letting people act in accordance with their religious principles, no matter what they might be, is to repudiate the power of reason, and to abdicate all moral responsibility. Reasons connected with human welfare hold anywhere.

ISLAMIC DRESS

Governments can sometimes object to the manifestation of religious belief because it is a public manifestation. The question then has to be what harm is being done. The wearing of distinctive Islamic dress by women illustrates this. The head-scarf was banned in French schools in 2004. Similar reasoning also led in Turkey to its being banned in the University of Istanbul. In both countries, the reasoning was that the assertion of religious identity in this way tended to undermine the ideal of the equality of everyone in a secular State. The position in Turkey was particularly sensitive, as is shown by the judgement on an appeal to the European Court of Human Rights by a university student from Istanbul. The case was subsequently referred to the Grand Chamber, where the original judgement was upheld by a majority of 16–1.[17] As the first Chamber makes clear, the question of religious dress was intimately related to the basic principle of the Turkish constitution that the State should be secular (*laick*).[18] People had been required to dress in accordance with their religious affiliations in the preceding Ottoman Empire, and the Turkish Constitutional Court feared that the adoption of the head-scarf as a religious duty would open up distinctions between practising Muslims, non-practising Muslims, and non-believers. Those who refused to wear the scarf would be seen as opposed to religion, and this could lead to tension.

The Chamber notes that for the Turkish Constitutional Court, outside the private sphere of the individual conscience, 'freedom to manifest one's religion could be restricted on public order grounds to defend the principle of secularism'.[19] Thus religious freedom becomes somewhat truncated, when put in the context of a society, which, perhaps for good reason, sees the public display of religious identity as a threat to the very existence of the State. The issue of which reasons can be given for the restriction of religious liberty becomes more difficult, once freedom is so related to context, that a particular government can decide how far it can be manifested in a particular society. A good reason in Turkey may not be a reason at all somewhere else.

The European Court is understandably reluctant to override decisions made nationally, saying in the same judgement that 'the national authorities are in principle better placed than an international court to evaluate local needs and conditions'.[20] A 'margin of appreciation' is to be left to such national authorities. This may be wise, since the traditions of countries recognizing the Court differ markedly. Turkey, as a secular State with an Islamic tradition, is different from traditionally Christian countries which have Established Churches. The Court recognized that Turkey's secularism may be necessary for the protection of the democratic system in Turkey, and upheld the ban on wearing the Islamic head-scarf in institutions of higher education.

How far should judgements be tailored to varying situations? If religious liberty is to mean anything, it cannot be given radically different interpretations depending on where you are. The needs of human nature remain constant. A judgement in London in the Court of Appeal, and reversed by the House of Lords in 2006,[21] was made soon after the first ruling on the Turkish case. It illustrates how legal opinions can vary on the same issue in a different context. The European Convention on Human Rights has been part of English law since the Human Rights Act of 1998, so the Turkish case was itself relevant. The Court was faced with an appeal concerning the right of a Muslim to wear, in a school with regulations about uniform, an Islamic dress (the *jilbab*), which covered her body apart from her face and hands. The school already allowed Islamic girls to wear some distinctive dress. The Court referred to the importance of context, mentioned by the European Court. Lord Justice Brooke in his judgement points out that the United Kingdom is not a secular State, and that religious education and collective worship is undertaken in schools.[22] It is, however, unclear what the relevance of this is to this case, since England is quite clearly not a Muslim State. There might be an issue about how far a predominantly Christian country should go in accommodating the wishes of a small section of the Muslim population. There should certainly be a presumption of religious freedom, to act in accordance with one's religious beliefs, but strains within the Muslim community itself, as well as the need to operate a cohesive school, may suggest that even a school with a large Muslim membership might be wise to be cautious about what it allows.

In this case, the Appeals Court came to the opposite conclusion from the European Court, and concluded that there had been an unlawful restriction on the right of the student to manifest her religion. There were legal objections to the school's method of decision-making.[23] It had not started with the view that the claimant had a right to manifest her religion, and then seen if there was sufficient reason for interfering with that right. It had merely decided on its uniform policy and expected it to be obeyed. The House of Lords was to take a very different view, holding that the school was fully justified. It had, Lord Bingham maintained, 'taken immense pains to devise a uniform policy which respected Muslim beliefs'. He believed that the school authorities were the people best placed to exercise judgement in such a matter.[24]

Larger issues, however, had emerged in the prior decision of the Court of Appeal. Lord Justice Scott Baker claimed that 'there is force in the criticism that it is not for school authorities to pick and choose between religious beliefs or shades of religious belief'.[25] They are all entitled to consideration under Article 9 of the European Convention. Lord Justice Brooke perhaps had a similar point in mind when he held:

There are clearly potential tensions between the rights and freedoms in a Convention agreed more than fifty years ago between West European countries which on the whole adhered to Judaeo-Christian traditions, and some of the tenets of the Islamic faith that relate to the position of women in society.[26]

This is a dangerous argument, which implies that when basic rights clash with Islamic tenets, this could be because of the background of the parties to agreements about rights. In other words, rights depend on agreements, not basic truths about human beings. This is to modify the idea of universal rights, and to suggest that reason is never going to suffice in recognizing them. It will always depend on whose reason.

There will always be scope for conflict between different rights which are laid down in charters and conventions. In this regard, religious freedom is no different, and can easily conflict with other demands which are explicit and implicit in bills of rights, such as the right to equal treatment, and freedom from discrimination. Religious demands made by some Muslims can easily conflict with issues about the equal treatment of women. Religious freedom is of exceptional importance, but it cannot be allowed automatically to trump other rights. A next step in arguments about uniform in schools could be a demand by some Muslim girls that they want their faces veiled. The problem is whether the mere assertion of a demand is enough to trigger the right to religious liberty. The temptation for the law is to extend religious freedom without making any assessment of what a religion is, or even what a reasonable request for special treatment might be. The courts are so anxious to avoid adjudicating on specifically religious issues, that 'religion' is treated indiscriminately. When sincerity is the only test a court is willing to make, even fanaticism may seem a recommendation. The fact that England is not a secular country apparently makes the Court feel it has to accept any claim stemming from any religion. Yet not all religion is the same.

Religious claims, even when stemming from recognized religions, cannot be accepted at face value. No country can allow religious liberty, the fruit of freedom, to be a means of attacking liberty. Just as there are limits beyond which a sect like the Amish should not reasonably be allowed to go, limits have to be placed on the activities of any religion. The European Convention recognizes this. It is significant that the examples which bring particular difficulty, whether in Christian Science, concerning Amish education, or the wearing of female Islamic dress, bear particularly on young people. Religion has an interest in teaching its faith, but a State also has to protect its young. The right to religious liberty, however precious, can never be so unqualified as to leave the lives of young people at the mercy of those who have contempt for the voice of reason.

RELIGIOUS FREEDOM AND THE LAW

Given the importance of religious freedom, there is always going to be the problem of its relation to the rule of law. Is the presumption to be that religion should be freely practised, unless there are strong reasons against, or, on the contrary, that laws apply equally to all, unless religions can gain exemptions? The result may often be the same, but the question of whether any religion should initially be above the law, and beyond its reach, is difficult. In a country with one traditional religion, one might not expect the law and religion to be antagonistic, although the religion may have claimed privileges. When there are many religions in a society, there may be clashes. Even though the law applies to all alike, it may still run foul of some religious conscience. One undoubted principle is that the rule of law is a way of promoting the common good. Favouritism, and arbitrary exceptions, in its application are to be deplored. This means that religious organizations should not be able to obtain exemption from the rule of law on the ground that they have their own disciplinary procedures. Even clergy have to be subject to the criminal law.

Notions about justice and impartiality are deeply rooted in much religion and in conceptions of God. The problem comes when many different groups want to shelter under the umbrella of religion and share its privileges. Judgements have to be made about the common interest. One writer says that when 'religious conduct harms others, accommodation is not consistent with the common good'.[27] We have seen that the need for religious liberty cannot 'trump' all possible considerations, but the problem is that what constitutes harm to others can be contested. On an issue, such as same-sex marriage, opposing views of society, and of what constitutes the common good, meet each other. This is why mere appeal to perceived harm cannot always settle the matter, and whatever a democracy decides to do, room has to be left for respecting people's consciences even when they are in the minority. Indeed, in complicated matters, the minority could one day be proved right, and their continuing fight for their principles may be valuable. The problem will be identifying the cases in which exemptions on grounds of conscience is justifiable. Just because there ought to be such cases does not change the fact that at times the harm done is obvious. There can then be less grounds for tolerating a religious practice, just because it is religious.

Is the default position, however, to be the rule of law, or religious liberty? Marci Hamilton suggests: 'The burden rests on the religious believer demanding exemption from a law to prove that his conduct is not harmful to the society and individuals within it'.[28] Speaking from an American experience, she holds that 'too many ill-considered exemptions have been granted, solely because the one demanding the exemption was religious'. She remarks that 'the result has been all manner of harm to women and children and property interests—and to the public good in general'. Yet who is to define 'harm' and 'public good'?

A major argument for special protection for religion follows from its exclusion from the public sphere, with the result that it cannot contribute directly to public debate. Since it cannot add its voice to arguments about harm and benefit, there may seem a point in giving it its own protected sphere. Once it is allowed to participate in public debate, using reasoning drawn from its own perspective but which might have a wider reson-ance, there may be less argument for exemptions, except when deep matters of conscience are at stake. It can contribute to public debate, and expect to be listened to. Even if it does not carry the day, it cannot object to the ensuing laws normally being applied to everyone. The separation of religion and public reason itself generates the dubious case for religion to be put in a special category and always to be treated differently.

4

Rights and Freedoms

DO RIGHTS COME FROM GOD?

THE IDEA of human rights is never far from any discussion about the public recognition of religion. It is a widespread commonplace that, in virtue of our common humanity, we all share the same basic rights, which have to be respected by everyone, and even incorporated into the law of the land. The United Nations Universal Declaration of Human Rights crystallized the issue in 1948 after the devastation of the Second World War. Article 18 deals with freedom of religion, and reads:

Everyone has the right to freedom of thought, conscience and religion; this right includes freedom to change his religion or belief, and freedom, either alone or in community with others and in public or private, to manifest his religion or belief in teaching, practice, worship and observance.[1]

This is the foundation of many charters of rights, including the European Convention on Human Rights. It was codified in the International Covenant on Civil and Political Rights, which eventually came into force in 1976. It is an aspiration that can attract widespread agreement, although there are still many parts of the world where such freedom is unknown. This makes the question of the basis of rights even more pressing. What are human rights, and where do they come from? A weak reply would be that such rights exist because the United Nations has agreed that they do. Is, though, that agreement to be explained simply in terms of the political atmosphere after a terrible war? If so, why are the rights claimed to be universal? The motivating idea is that the rights are unqualified. They do not only exist for the citizens of countries which are signatories to the Covenant, or which approved the original Declaration.

States do not create rights, but acknowledge them. Human rights are not mere civil rights. I may have a right to vote in my country. It does not follow that anyone who arrives in the United Kingdom should be immediately entitled to vote in a British election. On the other hand, anyone has a right to a fair trial, whoever they are. That springs from basic considerations of justice, not from particular citizenship. Not all rights and entitlements, recognized by particular governments, amount to human rights, and human rights cannot be met everywhere by one government. Governments have their special responsibilities, such as educating their own people. One of the problems about claims to human rights is that the rhetoric can be very unspecific about how they should be met. Clean water is very desirable for everyone, but we still need to know who has a particular responsibility for providing it in a particular place.

Rights which are absolute and of general application are easier to deal with, because everyone should respect them. A right not to be tortured need not specify who it is that should not torture you. No individual or State should. The claim to religious freedom is of this sort. All should respect the right to choose a religion. Yet this does not meet the question of what grounds such rights which apply everywhere. How do we decide what a right is, or what the force of calling something a right amounts to? It makes for powerful rhetoric, but the rhetoric can produce diminishing returns unless it is grounded in a properly articulated vision of the world and the place of humans in it.

A clear way of grounding rights itself came from religion. We each matter, it might be said, because we matter to God. This was the starting point of the Declaration of Independence by the United States of America in 1776. In its famous words, it declares that 'we hold these truths to be self-evident, that all men are created equal, that they are endowed by their Creator with certain inalienable rights'. Almost a century before in England, another revolution, the 'Glorious Revolution' of 1688, bloodlessly changed a regime in the name of rights in general, and of religious freedom in particular. One of its leading supporters, the philosopher, John Locke, wrote of 'natural rights', and conceived of 'natural obligation'. He had an incalculable influence on the founders of the United States. This may look a thoroughly secular view, but Locke wrote as an explicitly Christian philosopher. He said:

Ultimately, all obligation leads back to God, and we are bound to show ourselves obedient to the authority of his will because both our being and our work depend on his will ... moreover, it is reasonable that we should do what shall please him who is omniscient and most wise.[2]

The maker of rights and obligations is thus seen by Locke as a lawmaker, who knows what is best for us. At the same time, the 'rights of man' has often been seen as a secular battle-cry. Ideas of liberty and equality can be used against religion, as they were in the French Revolution. We still have to face the question of their grounding. Why is freedom to be respected, and human equality cherished? These questions have a ready answer in a religious context, since God, it will be held, has made us equal, cares for us equally, and has given us free-will so as to make reasoned choices. Once the religious context is subtracted, the mere existence of rights can seem more precarious. If agreements create them, why should they apply to those who are not parties to the agreement? What justifies such an agreement? The universality, which seems inseparable from the idea of human rights, suggests a metaphysical view encompassing all human beings, whatever the contingent political facts may be at any given time.

THE IMPORTANCE OF TOLERATION

The problem of the status of rights becomes more acute when we see how rights are codified in the law of particular jurisdictions. In one sense, the more general problem becomes irrelevant when the full force of the law of a country is applied. The issue then appears to be a legal, rather than a philosophical, one. Nevertheless the idea of a right very often lacks specificity, and is under-determined. It may be a fine aspiration, but it is often unclear what it amounts to in practical terms. It has to take on life in the context of a particular legal system. Interpretation, application and growing precedent flesh out what is a very bare bone.

What criteria can be used to give meaning to the demand for religious liberty? Such a question cannot be divorced from the issue of why such liberty matters. Locke himself was in no doubt. He says in 'An Essay on Toleration' that 'purely speculative' opinions, such as belief in the Trinity, should be matters on which individuals should have freedom to decide.[3] There should also be an 'unlimited toleration' on 'the place, time and manner of worshipping my God'. Locke's reason is that 'this is between God and me'. It is a matter of a concern for eternity, and should be beyond the reach of politics and government 'which are but for my well being in this world'. Locke's reasoning is theological, since he sees the way to personal salvation as not being 'any forced, exterior performance, but the voluntary and secret choice of the mind'.[4] Given that God wishes us to use our freedom to choose to obey Him, Locke stresses that it should not be thought that 'men should give the magistrate a power to choose for them their way to salvation'.

Freedom is thus seen as given to humans by God. If we choose not to exercise it ourselves, and submit to an external authority, we are not acting in accordance with God's will. Similarly we may wish to restrict other people's freedom to choose their religious beliefs, but if we do, we are undermining the basis for religion, and not supporting it. Freedom of worship, and indeed the freedom to choose one's religion lie at the root of what religion is about. Coerced religion is not genuine religion, and is not pleasing to God. That at least is what Locke concludes from his own Christian belief. When what he refers to as 'infinite happiness or infinite misery' is at stake, men are not going to be turned from what they themselves think best, whatever 'the magistrate's' ruling.[5]

Locke's views stem from a Christian belief that our choices in this life determine our eternal destiny. This life is but part of a wider whole. It is crucial that they are our own choices, for which we are fully responsible. The idea of judgement presupposes a prior freedom. We cannot be blamed for that which we have been coerced into doing. Our freedom, indeed, mirrors, Locke thought, the freedom of God, who could have chosen to create the world in many different ways. Locke was reflecting the stress on free will, and its importance for moral responsibility and for the exercise of reason, which was made by the so-called 'Cambridge Platonists'. One of them was Benjamin Whichcote, previously Provost of King's College, Cambridge. Locke attended his church in London, St Lawrence Jewry, after the Restoration of the monarchy, and would have regularly heard him preach there.

This view of freedom was not one which would have been held by strict Puritans under Cromwell, during the English Civil War and Commonwealth, or those who founded the 'Commonwealth' of Massachusetts. They believed in a God who chose his 'elect', and they preached the sovereignty of Christ over a godly Commonwealth. Religious liberty was a threat to that vision. Diversity would undermine the godliness and holiness of the whole. Even though they wanted to escape the domination of the Church of England, they wanted to replace it with a new Establishment, which allowed no dissent. In Boston, Massachusetts, in 1659, for example, the Quaker, Mary Dyer, and two others, were condemned to death for their beliefs.

Locke lived through all the convulsions of civil war in England, and had seen its terrible effects. He later gave financial support to the Duke of Monmouth, whose rebellion in 1685 against the Catholic King, James II, came to a swift end at the Battle of Sedgemoor. Locke was in exile in Holland, and only able to return to England, with Queen Mary, when William and Mary ascended the throne. The Battle of Sedgemoor had taken place in Locke's own native county of Somerset, and those who took part in the rebellion were cruelly punished by Judge Jefferies, the Lord Chief Justice. His 'Bloody Assizes' have never been forgotten, and Jefferies' name is still held in contempt in the West of England. It is significant that twelve men were hanged in Locke's home village of Pensford. Violence, with its roots in religious bigotry, came very close to home for Locke.

The devastation of civil war in England had a profound effect on the thinking of those who lived through it, and it had its effect on philosophical thought. An emphasis on the importance of reason, not violence, in settling disputes, together with the stress on a God-given freedom, provided a fabric for a society in which differences could be respected and lived with. Enforced agreement was always going to be impossible, and Locke says trenchantly that it had certainly not preserved the Church of England, nor hindered the growth of Puritanism. He adds:

If, therefore, violence be to settle uniformity, tis in vain to mince the matter. The severity which must produce it cannot stop short of the total destruction and extirpation of all dissenters at once.[6]

He suggests that this is hardly in accordance with Christian doctrine, and that the Massacre of the Huguenots, French Protestants, in France in 1572 should not be imitated. Liberty and tolerance were the only alternative to a path which would inevitably lead to persecution, violence, civil war and widespread death. He is saying all this not as a sceptical onlooker, despairing of religion, but from the point of view of a committed Christian, a worshipping member of the Church of England. He was in that Church in fact a forerunner of those who were to be called 'latitudinarians', and, as we have seen, he himself used the newly coined term 'latitudinism'.[7] He wanted to make the doctrinal pre-conditions for belonging to a broadly based Church as wide as possible, to include and not exclude, and perhaps only demanding the simple acceptance that Jesus was the Messiah.[8] He had little patience with arguments which threatened to split the Church over what was of less than major importance. He felt that the government should not be allowed to intervene in 'indifferent matters', as Parliament undoubtedly did in the Established Church. He says:

Kneeling or sitting in the sacrament can itself tend no more to the disturbance of the government or injury of my neighbour than sitting or standing at my own table; wearing a cope or surplice in the church can no more in its own nature alarm or threaten the peace of the state than wearing a cloak or coat in the market.[9]

Whether the State should intervene in such questions is not of course the same issue as whether a Church could comprehend differences or must split. If the latter, the State then has to face the question how far it should tolerate the existence of different Churches. In the end, parliamentary control over the Church of England remained, but 'nonconformists' or 'dissenters' were allowed to worship in their own way in their own chapels. A more tolerant and inclusive Church might have produced less schism, but the basic issue of the role of the State in its relations with the Church was itself a contentious issue.

Locke wanted toleration both within the Church of England and beyond it. Yet his own views about religious liberty had their limits. He refused toleration to atheists, not least because they could make no sense, he thought, of human equality.[10]

His starting point was that no laws should be made or restraints established 'unless the necessity of the state and the welfare of the people called for them'.[11] This leaves room for debate about what would constitute a necessity, or what is demanded by people's welfare. In spirit, however, this caveat is not so very different from that entered in modern charters of rights such as the European Convention.

As we have previously seen, once limits are mentioned, it becomes clear that rights cannot be absolute. Locke recognized the difficulty in practical situations of always observing a right. He was reluctant to tolerate Roman Catholics because they were not themselves tolerant. This was part of the continuing conundrum of how far a liberal and tolerant society can tolerate intolerance. Locke firmly said that 'papists are not to enjoy the benefits of toleration, because where they have the power, they think themselves bound to deny it to others'.[12] He also felt that posed a danger to the general welfare, in that their loyalty was ultimately to the Pope, embodying a foreign jurisdiction, and not to their own government. They must therefore be considered 'irreconcilable enemies', on the ground that their opinions 'are absolutely destructive to all governments but the pope's'.

This was written at a time when Catholicism and power politics were inextricably linked, and the painful divisions of the Reformation still reverberated across Europe. The antagonism between Protestants and Catholics was itself a sign of the terrible dangers of too close a relationship between the spiritual realm and the world of politics. Once religion was harnessed for political purposes, hell could indeed be let loose. Locke himself somewhat pessimistically remarks that 'the Christian religion hath made more factions, wars and disturbances in civil societies than any other'.[13] Whether that was true then, and continues to be so, could be a matter for much historical debate. It must certainly have seemed to an Englishman of the late seventeenth century that his country had been torn apart by religious differences. Even if religion was not the sole cause, religious differences had contributed to the Civil War, and the result was nothing but death and destruction.

Whatever Locke's views of the effects of Christian disunity, his vision of a tolerant society was based on Christian doctrine. He saw atheism as dangerous on the grounds that it removed the basis of society. Belief in God is, he claims, 'the foundation of all morality' influencing 'the whole life and actions of men'.[14] Without morality we are like animals and incapable of society. The fact of human freedom is, of course, closely linked with the possibility of moral responsibility, and Locke was also convinced of the existence of a natural equality between all humans. That idea had enormous political implications, and suggested that the power of a sovereign lay not in some divine right, but in the agreement of those on whose behalf he or she ruled. There lay the foundation of a notion of a constitutional monarchy, existing to uphold the laws, and to govern fairly and impartially.

That was the framework established in 1689 in England after the Glorious Revolution. Yet its idea of equality was a Christian one. God created us, Locke says, in 'a state...of equality, wherein all the power and jurisdiction is reciprocal, no one having more than another'.[15] This view of a natural equality is linked to the idea that we are each free and endowed with what Locke calls 'the light of reason...natural and implanted in men'. Such notions form the foundations of modern democracy, but they are often wrenched from their theological context and left to stand on their own, with the unargued assumption that this does not change anything.

WHY ARE WE ALL EQUAL?

The conception of a basic natural equality is taken for granted in many discussions of human rights. On it depends the conviction that all humans should matter equally, and be treated equally in matters of justice and fairness. Some would see these assertions as self-evident, but that is largely because of the tradition which has nurtured us. In many places, such ideas are still rejected. Locke saw equality as God-given, and our recognition of it as the out-working of a natural reason which is itself grounded in God. Indeed in the slogan beloved of the Cambridge Platonists, and used by Locke himself, reason is 'the candle of the Lord'.[16] The early Enlightenment, with its stress on reason, and on empirical science as an expression of it, was still grounded in a religious understanding of the world. The crunch question is how far a reliance on reason, and beliefs in equality and freedom, can survive if that basis is removed. The eighteenth-century Enlightenment in France thought that they could. The current 'post-modern' reaction against the 'modern' idea of reason indicates that such confidence may be misplaced.

One contemporary writer on legal and political theory comments: 'Although there is plenty of work on equality, there is precious little in the modern literature on the background idea that we humans, are, fundamentally, one another's equals.'[17] He points out that this is not because the fundamental principle is considered unimportant, but just that most writing presupposes its importance. He concludes:

Rights and Freedoms

Among those who make use of some very basic principle of human equality, virtually no-one has devoted much energy to explaining what the principle amounts to in itself, nor . . . to the task of outlining what the refutation of any serious philosophical denial of basic equality would have to involve.[18]

It is too often taken for granted that we are all equal, and debates immediately concentrate on the practical application of the principle. Should we, for instance, concentrate on equality of opportunity, or press for equality of outcome? How egalitarian a society should we strive for in matters of economics? What does equal treatment of people of different sex, race, religion, sexual orientation and so on demand? These are debates at the heart of contemporary law and politics. There are few in Western societies who might be prepared to say that, in principle, we are not all of equal worth. Yet this current unanimity of view has not been held throughout history, and is certainly not believed everywhere today. It may be the basic tenet of democratic society, and indeed the justification for democracy, but its rationale is usually left vague. In Locke's day, it certainly was not taken for granted. For instance, the principle of the divine right of kings had been articulated and was still held by some. Only by challenging that principle could a new constitutional settlement in England, with a Bill of Rights, become feasible.

From a philosophical point of view, Nietzsche's attacks in the nineteenth century on the idea of human equality, and his extolling of 'higher and lower men' provide a warning that in modern times the idea of equality has not been unquestioned, even in Western Europe.[19] He was an implacable opponent of Christianity and its morality, thinking it was a device by the weak to hold back the strong. Seen as an early apostle of post-modernism, Nietzsche believed that, once Christian metaphysics was removed from the scene, equality could no longer be taken for granted. The project of finding a rational basis for equality is not an irrelevant academic exercise. When challenged, it is crucial that we can articulate reasons why all humans are equal. It must be more than the prejudice of time and place, and the necessary assumption of Western democracy. Otherwise, we are in a poor state to advocate democracy to sceptics in other parts of the world, or to defend it against critics at home. Equality is written into all our views about the functioning of public life. It was part of the slogan of the French Revolution—*liberté, egalité, fraternité*. It is an assumption of utilitarian moral and political philosophy, with its assumption that everyone counts as one in any calculus of costs and benefits for the general good. More particularly, it is the foundation of every idea of human rights, with their claim to universality.

From a historical point of view, ideas of equality certainly grew on Christian soil. The idea that we are all equal, in the sight of the God who created us, has been powerful. From God's point of view, it has been claimed, all differences of rank, social position, and so on are irrelevant. We are all God's children. The French slogan itself can be given a theological underpinning, although in 1789 such ideas were torn out of that context. Nevertheless it could be said that we should be free, because freedom is the gift of God, who has given us free will, which we should be allowed to exercise. Similarly, the argument is that we are equal, because God loves us all equally. We thus should recognize we are 'brothers' because we all share the same Heavenly Father. Indeed the notion of 'fraternité' makes little sense outside that specific context.

The fashion today is for rhetoric about human rights to ignore the need for any justification, let alone a theological one. It sometimes seems that human rights exist because people say that they do. People matter because we choose to think that. We are equal because that is how we treat each other. The inadequacy of this should be clear. Rights then depend for their implementation on political agreements which may or may not last. There seems to be no way of justifying them, and little reason to transmit them to future generations. The theological justification remains in the background, sometimes invoked, but more often ignored.

How much should we rely on the theological justification? We can certainly ignore it, and hope that we can keep the superstructure without the historical foundation. That is probably not very feasible, and, in that case, we may have to change other beliefs about the importance of human beings, seeing, for example, no principled distinction between humans and animals. Some welcome that, but if we wish to retain our belief in the importance of humanity, and the 'sanctity' of human life, we may have to stress the role of religion in educational systems, and in the public sphere generally. So far from being privatized, it would turn out that religion was explicitly required to explain our intuitions about how our society should be organized. To say that in the current Western world this is controversial would be an understatement.

THE PRIMACY OF THE INDIVIDUAL

Talk of equality refers to individuals, and human rights themselves are normally regarded as attributes of individuals.

Religion, and Christianity in particular, may preach the worth of individuals, as we have seen, but it cannot itself be reduced to individual belief. It claims truth, and collectively guards that truth in organized religion, attempting within the community of believers to put it into practice. The way in which modern law attempts to protect individuals so that they can exercise their rights, and be protected from discrimination, can put greater stress on the role of an individual, and his or her rights, than on the importance of respecting communities. It thus can ignore the communal aspect of religion, by giving priority to the role of each individual. Even truth itself is seen as a matter of individual beliefs about what is true, with the state claiming total neutrality. Indeed if this is taken to its logical conclusion, equality and freedom are seen as the 'values' of individuals, and not part of the assumptions of the State. At this point things become incoherent, since the State is adopting a neutrality about certain 'values' in the name of those values.

In fact, a Western, liberal, view of society has to take a stand on some substantive issues.[20] Ideas of freedom and equality have to underpin our law. Yet the tendency is to see society as made up of individuals and not groups or communities. The assumption is that individuals must decide for themselves what is to matter for them, and that it cannot be imposed. Justice is often seen as justice to individuals, without regard for the traditions of communities. This is illustrated by the Canadian *Charter of Rights and Freedoms* of 1982. It is a classic document about human rights which has influenced other jurisdictions. Article 15 deals with equality, and states:

Every individual is equal before and under the law and has the right to equal protection and equal benefit of the law without discrimination, and, in particular, without discrimination based on race, national or ethnic origin, colour, religion, sex, age, or mental or physical ability.[21]

The individualist stress is clear. What matters is the equality of individuals. The drafters saw this, and drew back slightly in the second clause of the article, which expressly allows 'any law, program or activity', which is intended to ameliorate the 'conditions of disadvantaged individuals or groups', thus allowing programmes of affirmative action. These are often controversial because people are judged not on their own merits, but on the basis of their membership of a group, whether racial, religious, or whatever. People could then be given advantages because of their racial background, and some would see that as inherently racist.

The tug between the demand and rights of individuals, and those of communities, can be real enough, as battles over the place of the French language in Quebec have long illustrated. Article 27 of the *Charter* insists that it be interpreted 'in a manner consistent with the preservation and enhancement of the multicultural heritage of Canadians'.[22] Individual rights have to be judged against the need to preserve cultures, which of their nature are collective. In this, as much else, the *Charter* has to be interpreted through Canadian law. Its practical effects depend on the courts, and, in particular, the Canadian Supreme Court. Noble aspirations, and vague phrases, have to be given concrete expression.

Reference to groups and cultures makes it clear that law has to be applied to a diverse society, defined by its multicultural condition. The *Charter* aims to provide a framework which assumes diversity and disagreement, and defines how people can live together in spite of that. Yet the very notions of equality and freedom cannot themselves be contested, and must be respected in a society which continues to nurture them. Diversity, at the extreme, could destroy the very means by which it can be tolerated. We have seen how the rhetoric of human rights can float free of rational grounding. In the same way, legal documents about rights, applying to specific societies, tend to float free of any recognizable grounding in a historically situated society. Indeed a culture of rights can be nurtured within specific traditions, and as a result of specific religious beliefs, such as those of John Locke. Then appeals to those rights on an individual basis can begin to destroy the possibility of transmitting the beliefs on which they are grounded.

The demand that laws should not discriminate on grounds of religion opens the way for a conscious separation of all religion from the apparatus of the State, and its laws. It may be argued that once a State appeals to the assumptions and beliefs of any particular religion, it allies itself with that religion. The claim is that it makes citizens subscribing to other religions or none feel as if they are not full members of that society. This is a recurring theme. The structure of human rights enforcement, with its concentration on the individual, and not on the cultural context, provides such a process with an irresistible force. The idea that all humans are of equal importance implies, it seems, that each individual must be seen in abstraction. Not only are characteristics such as race to be properly ignored, but religion is to be regarded as irrelevant. This is not just a matter of not favouring those with some beliefs, or victimizing others. A belief in religious freedom ought to guard against that. The argument seems to be that to avoid any appearance of discrimination, the State must keep its distance, and not identify itself with beliefs which only some of its citizens may hold.

Assuming that religious belief is on a par with issues about race is misleading. A state should be 'colour-blind' with regard to the racial origins of its citizens. Should it, by analogy be 'religion-blind', in the sense that it should officially have no view about religion, which should be regarded as a purely individual matter? The problem is that, as we have seen, the idea that we should all be equal has definite historical roots in religion. Religion, too, can provide the rational grounding of which ideas about equality and freedom are in need. Insisting that, in the name of a principle of equality which has been derived from religion, the state must be separated from religion, appears paradoxical. It could even be destroying the foundations on which the edifice has been built.

Rights cannot be advocated in a vacuum. Total neutrality by a State implies indifference as to whether rights should be respected. There will always have to be a positive programme of education to create an atmosphere in which laws can be enforced. Even a liberal State, preoccupied with the rights of individuals, has to ensure that children are brought up to value them. The problem is that the importance of respecting particular rights begins to undermine any idea of why the rights were regarded as important in the first place. For example, the importance of religious liberty is seen as implying that each person is free to believe anything. It will then seem wrong to imply that some beliefs are better established than others, because that is to cast judgement on the decisions of individuals. The State could seem to be challenging their freedom. Diversity is not just a consequence, but is celebrated as good in itself, as the proper result of freedom. Rational debate about religion is then seen not as the proper implementation of that freedom, but as an assault on individual rights. If people are being told they are wrong in what they believe, especially by views which appear to have official backing, that is held to be an attack on the values of freedom and equality. Not only are some setting themselves up above others, but the State could be using its authority and power to champion a particular view.

We thus quickly travel along a route which takes us far from Locke's Christian arguments for a tolerant society. A society which upholds the importance of the individual because of its Christian heritage changes into a secular one, seeing Christianity as one option amongst many. Yet the unsettling thing is that it does so because of principles which are rooted in Christianity. Instead of recognizing the roots of such presuppositions, all official activities, and all public life, have to be cleansed of any suspicion of support for one religion rather than another. All beliefs have to be equally valued, because it is feared that the holders of such beliefs, and the adherents of different religions (and of none) will not feel equally valued by the State. Because of a commendable desire to ensure that people of different faiths can live together, the State seems to conclude that it does not matter which one is held. Indeed it does not matter whether one rejects all religion. This message is then transmitted through its educational system. A Christian nation, for reasons of Christian principle, stemming from a belief in what is seen as our God-given equality and freedom, becomes a secular nation, committed to no religion. This is no theoretical conjecture of what might happen. It is the course taken by Canada, at least in its legal system, since 1982 and the introduction of the *Charter of Rights and Freedoms.* It is the course being increasingly followed elsewhere, even in the United Kingdom, because of the pressure from human rights legislation.

5

Multiculturalism and Religion

CULTURE AND THE INDIVIDUAL

ARE INDIVIDUALS or communities to be the bearer of rights? The freedom of individuals, and their rights, can clash with the demands of a multiculturalist programme. Encouraging cultural diversity may produce different results from giving priority to individual freedom. In both cases the State can be neutral towards the content of beliefs. Yet this itself raises the question how far a State can exist as a coherent entity without itself setting standards through its laws, and through the beliefs it transmits within its educational system. A State holding no beliefs cannot uphold freedom and toleration. This is, of course, to treat a 'State' as itself a continuing entity, and some would hold that it has no existence apart from the individuals who make it up. They would say that States do not have beliefs, because only individuals do.

Is a society ever anything more than a combination of the separate beliefs and understandings of the individuals who make it up?[1] Are we isolated 'atoms', happening to combine in society, but having a nature that precedes joining any community? On the other hand, is our identity created by the societies, and cultures, into which we are born? The answer to these questions is central to our understanding of the role of religion. The relationship between a society, or a culture, and religion is never accidental, but a defining feature. Even an atheist country such as Soviet Russia gained much of its character from opposition to religion. Cultures within wider societies are also typically moulded by their relationships with particular religions. When individuals form their beliefs, they are often influenced not just by the beliefs they adopt, but by the ones they reject. A thinker such as Nietzsche, to whom Christianity was anathema, was the son of a Lutheran pastor. The God he regarded as dead was the Christian God.

Those who want to respect, and encourage, cultural diversity in the present age, very often reject individualist assumptions. They do not see the need to foster the autonomy of individuals, because they see the important differences as operating at the level of culture. Whatever else such 'cultures' might be, with their assortment of distinctive beliefs and practices, and different languages and religions, they are shared by groups, and serve to identify them. Many want to preserve autonomy at the level of groups and institutions. They look to preserving and encouraging different ways of life, and not just the choices of individuals. I am, they would say, who I am, not because of some basic nature, but am formed by the community into which I am born.

There is an implicit relativism in this, because it tends to stress that different groups occupy different compartments, each with their own standards. The result is to advocate the protection of ways of life as such within the State. Whereas a liberal might see individual choice and personal commitment as of paramount importance, others would see the existence of a range of cultures as evidence of genuine freedom. They offer genuinely alternative styles of life, when they exist autonomously within a neutral State. Such a view may surreptitiously admit that the possibility of individual choice between such alternatives is important. It also points out that choice in a vacuum is meaningless. Without the transmission of ideas and practices through a communal culture there will be nothing left for individuals to choose. Liberalism as an ideal itself does not miraculously begin afresh with each new generation.

Too much emphasis on the freedom of the individual can lead us to forget the importance of the cultural dimension. The assumptions and practices of the society we are born into will always influence and constrain our choices. We may be free to repudiate them, but they will always provide the raw material with which we begin to shape our lives. A multicultural delight in diversity can encourage the view that the existence of difference, rather than uniformity, somehow aids us in our choices. Yet there is a difference between a principled belief in the autonomy of cultures as whole entities, and the more individualist idea that diversity widens options for individuals.

CULTURAL DIVERSITY OR PERSONAL FREEDOM?

Once the priority of culture over the individual is taken seriously, the flourishing of different cultures and institutions becomes vital. The liberal stress on individual autonomy, seen particularly in the rhetoric of human rights, is alleged to erode the role of traditional cultures and religions. Many would challenge the idea of religious freedom, in the sense of individuals being able to opt out of cultures and religions, and make their own choice. Once it is accepted that society, and culture, moulds the person, rather than the other way round, it makes nonsense to consider any individual breaking free of the very context which has provided meaning, and identity. Bhikhu Parekh, writing on 'multiculturalism' spells this out. He says: 'Since culture is concerned with the meaning and significance of human activities and relations, and since this is a matter of central concern to religion, the two tend to be closely connected.'[2] He points out that 'cultural communities are not voluntary associations like clubs, political parties and pressure groups'.[3] They are not means to other ends but are communities lasting through history. Indeed the most salient fact about culture is that it comprises what can be taught and passed on. Parekh claims that 'unlike voluntary associations, we are deeply shaped by our cultural communities, and derive our ideals and values from them'.[4] He believes that it follows that we cannot leave them in the same way we can simply resign from a voluntary association. The influence of a community will continue to be felt, as it was in the extreme case of Nietzsche as he rejected Christianity and flirted with nihilism.

A belief in the primacy of culture will make cultural diversity seem important, because a refusal to allow one culture to dominate others is considered more fundamental than individual freedom. This would follow from the relativism endemic in the position. There would be no idea of truth, or of transcultural standards, for cultures to meet. Preference for any particular culture would then seem arbitrary. The great danger is that even our common humanity is forgotten, as alleged differences between cultures are extolled to the detriment of any idea of the nature we all share. All this throws in sharp relief the problem of what constitutes religious freedom, and how important organizations, such as Churches, should be. Should the focus of law be to protect the freedom of individuals, or to foster the autonomy of religious groups? A stress on human rights would lead to protecting individual freedom. One on cultural rights might champion the demands of an organized religion on its members. What grounds, it might be said, are there for the law of the State to interfere with the internal beliefs and practices of a religion?

Nowhere is the clash clearer than in arguments over whether a member of a religion should have the right to leave it. One of the most basic freedoms that any human can have, if not the most basic, would seem to be the right to choose one's religion. That must inevitably include the right to give it up, even if one had been born into it. Yet if culture is the source of my identity, would I still be me if I repudiated my cultural background by giving up the religion which helped form me?

Kwame Anthony Appiah, a philosopher at Princeton, raises the question whether 'it really makes sense to say that you can exit an identity group'.[5] He adds that 'as ex-Mormons like to point out, being an ex-Mormon has itself become a kind of ethnicity'. There have been many philosophical arguments about the nature of the self, and they go to the heart of problems about the relation of individuals to the society which nurtured them. How much of my history could be taken away and still leave 'me'? In this connection, Appiah asks: 'If the unencumbered self is a myth, how can you extricate yourself from the context that confers meaning?' He points out that no-one can 'exit' their language, especially if it is their only one. Yet this brings us back to the issue of freedom. I can hardly have any free will if I cannot choose what is most important for me. The stress on culture as the only formative factor can make it impossible to escape from any part of it, not least religion. I certainly could obtain no rational grounds for doing so, because there would be nowhere for me to stand in order to weigh reasons. I would either be inside the religion accepting it, or outside, inevitably failing to understand it properly.

The law of any country has to decide if it is going to protect the individual's conscience or the rights of a community. These may not be alternatives, but they sometimes are. Certainly in the case of the Amish, the preservation of a way of life was seen as more important than the need to give a high school education to children. Appiah himself refers to those who, particularly in the context of arguments within the United States, do not see the autonomy of the individual conscience as the whole of religious freedom. As he says, they believe that 'the claims of the religious institution against the state rather than the claims of the individual dissenter as such, must be taken as primary'.[6] One argument given for this, he points out, is that 'the state that accommodates religion has accepted an important check on its own power'.

The issue of the preservation of the standards of a religion can often cut across individual rights. A religion may want the whole society to abide by its standards, and many will resent that. At the same time, leaving everything to individual choice may make a mockery of a religion being able to live by its own standards, when confronted by a society which does not want to uphold them. This problem is given concrete expression, as we shall see, in disputes about the observation of the Sabbath. In predominantly Christian countries, there are going to be problems about the use of Sunday. A paradox may well be that individual Christians can only make Sunday a special day if the whole society sees it that way.

Whether people wish to worship is up to the individual. Whether there is space for public worship depends on how society is organized. A State that is 'neutral' in its laws about such matters will in practice become a place in which people will often have to choose between their jobs and keeping Sunday free for worship. A social climate will be produced in which worship and rest on a common day for all is not regarded as relevant consideration. There may be no neutral ground for a nation between underwriting certain religious priorities on a collective basis, and pursuing an aggressively secular agenda, which may seem hostile to particular religious practices.

This type of case suggests that there has to be a cultural and social dimension for religious practice. No religion is only practised individually. Otherwise it could be whatever a believer wanted it to be, and questions of truth drop out. Practitioners need to join with others. In the case of Christianity, this is certainly so. A Christian who makes no attempt to be in contact with fellow Christians, even to worship with them, is hardly following Christian tradition.

Does this suggest that culture always exists first, and that individuals come second? Since part of Christian tradition, at least, is the importance of the individual conscience, this is going too far. Some adherents of Islam resist such notions of freedom, on the grounds that ideas of freedom of choice have their roots in Western thought and are alien to their religion. This shows itself particularly in that for some Muslims, religious freedom cannot include the right to change religion. A Muslim cannot, some would hold, commit 'apostasy' and leave the religion. This is the reason some Islamic countries are reluctant to adhere to international conventions on human rights, because they assume that the ability to change one's religion, and to reject a particular one, must be a corner-stone of religious freedom. Article 18 of the United Nations Universal Declaration, of 1948, explicitly says that freedom of conscience and religion, includes the freedom of someone 'to change his religion or belief'.[7] Saudi Arabia objected to this on the grounds that this was prohibited under Islamic law.

There has been a tendency for some Muslim scholars to see religious freedom as simply the right of non-Muslims to remain under Islamic rule without interference. Religious conversion from Islam (and preaching by other religions to Muslims) was forbidden. This is all a matter of ongoing dispute within Islam, particularly when Islamic countries are subjected to pressure by those demanding human rights. Two Muslim writers conclude that 'one of the new positions emerging among many Muslims today is that the Qur'an supports the view that freedom of belief is an essential aspect of Islam'.[8] It remains to be seen whether this will be generally seen as the rediscovery of a genuine strand in traditional Islam, or a forlorn attempt to make it conform to the pressures of the modern world.

CULTURE OR CONTRACT?

The stress on the priority of community, with laws against apostasy, can arise from the need to hold a community together. The ensuing idea that cultural diversity is to be encouraged, and other cultures respected, goes further than mere toleration. It suggests that a culture, exemplified perhaps by a religion, is valuable in itself, since it is the source of meaning for its adherents. Yet those advocating a multicultural approach, and upholding cultural diversity and social differences, do so in an apparently rational way. They appear to stand outside all cultures, and to judge their importance in a neutral and detached manner. They can rise above the constraints of their own culture, even if no-one else can. They seem to be able to survey things as they are, and then pass judgement on the central role culture plays in people's lives. They judge the value of diversity. Yet their approach stems from the assumption that we are each formed by our culture, and cannot step outside it.

The assertion of multiculturalism shows by its very possibility that all this is far from the case. We are each rational, and able to make judgements about truth, whatever powerful social influences have been working on us. The fact that anyone can argue for multiculturalism gives the lie to it in any strong form. This is not to deny the importance of culture in inclining us one way or another. We cannot be indifferent to our social climate. In the end, however, anyone can break free of any tradition in search of truth. We are not wholly conditioned by our surroundings. Personal freedom is the precondition for any proper reasoning, and it is reasoning that makes the proclamation possible of multiculturalism itself.

The mere celebration of different cultures, and religions, results in an unwillingness to take the claims of any of them seriously. This is particularly so in the case of religion. In a sense, no-one can live outside all culture, and multiculturalism itself encourages a particular kind of culture. It may even constitute one, and can inadvertently become an attack on all religion. If there is no particular reason for belonging to one religion rather than another, other than it is 'mine', there may seem little reason for any continuing commitment to it, particularly if it makes inconvenient demands.

Faced with different religions and cultures, perhaps as a result of significant immigration, one option might appear to be the one adopted by France. As we shall see, it removes all religion from the public stage. Individuals and communities can practise their own religion, but it must not impinge on the life of the secular State. The latter makes no pretence to be officially multicultural, but the result is that all religion seems less important than what is publicly acknowledged, and publicly taught in schools. As a result, such toleration may not seem enough for different cultures and religions. They may be tolerated, but toleration often stems from a respect for freedom, rather than any approval. I do not merely tolerate what I admire. Different cultures and religions press for more than this from their society. They want positive acceptance through official recognition.

Communities want the collective rights which they see as following from this. How far, though, can collectivities, whether Churches or other groups, claim the same kind as individuals? The law can and does recognize the rules of particular organizations, but as applying internally, not making any claims which could affect others outside. M. H. Ogilvie, a Canadian lawyer, writes with particular reference to Canadian tradition:

Since the common law regards religious institutions as voluntary organisations, self-governed by contract, the courts defer to the laws and customs of religious institutions, enforcing these except where some internal irregularity has occurred or the rules of natural justice have not been applied.[9]

Multiculturalism and Religion

Courts in Western countries have been traditionally reluctant to become involved (or 'entangled') in doctrinal and theological disputes. They will make rulings about the ownership of property in the event of schism by applying the rules of the institution concerned. They will not take sides in whatever doctrinal disputes have brought about the schism. The basis of this, in those countries influenced by England, is the tradition of common law. That typically views religious organizations, such as Christian denominations, as collections of individuals, whose members have entered into a contract or covenant with each other. The position of an Established Church will be different, but in other cases the issue will involve the enforcing of a contract. Schism will be treated in the same way as if members of a golf club fall out and dispute the ownership of the club. The courts have to make a decision, based on the interpretation of the rules of the club. Wider national and social considerations will be irrelevant. Individuals have made an agreement, which must be upheld in all its particulars.

This picture is one of individuals banding together under the supervision of the common law. It is not one of a multicultural society, in which all cultures and religions themselves can determine what is just, and have their own rules and laws. According to a strong multiculturalism, one cannot judge from outside that particular cultures and religions have gone beyond what is acceptable. A practice such as polygamy could not be condemned from outside the religion practising it. Similarly, the law would never be in a position to judge that a culture ignores individual liberty. Yet assumptions about the importance of such liberty have animated the common law since the days of King John and Magna Carta, signed at

Runnymede in 1215. Against any belief in personal freedom, a stress on the formative role of culture means that it takes precedence over the individual. Culture is viewed, not as the product of some contract, but as the root of a person's identity. It follows that beliefs about the value of each individual reflect particular cultural beliefs, such as those of Christianity.

Yet all this stops us referring, as Professor Ogilvie does, to 'natural justice'. Even such a basic concept comes from a tradition of law imbued with Christian assumptions. In a multicultural society, such talk would be seen as culturally biased, if it attempted to apply ideas of justice and freedom across the board, perhaps insisting on the rights of women, even when religions ignored them. Yet it is impossible to govern a society unless everyone is treated impartially according to the same principles. That is the rule of law.

A multicultural society of the kind envisaged can appeal to nothing in common between cultures. The ideal of human equality is suspect because it must assume constancy of 'human' nature across cultures. While it may be trivially true that all cultures are human, it will be said, they mediate and express that nature in different ways. Parekh claims that 'we cannot ground equality in human uniformity because the latter is inseparable from, and ontologically no more important than, human differences'.[10] He is explicitly opposed to granting equality on the basis of a shared human nature, while denying it 'at the equally important cultural level'.[11] This goes to the heart of the issue of how far individuals gain their identity through a culture, and how far they should even on occasion be protected from it.

The idea of a common human nature as the ground for our respect for each other is of immense importance. Culture and social factors can be emphasized to the point of ignoring our humanity. As a result, people will retreat both literally and figuratively, into cultural ghettos, with no reason to respect the members of other cultures and religions. There is no common ground, whether in the shape of an appeal to human nature, or the equally important question of a common world we all live in. To the relativist, even the latter can only be interpreted through the concepts of different systems of belief, with no common point of reference.[12]

Parekh reaches that point, and argues against any 'monistic' view of what is good for humans. He says that it produces the following sequence:

Since human beings are supposed to be basically the same, only a particular way of life is deemed to be worthy of them, and those failing to live up to it either do not merit equality or do so only after they are suitably civilized. The idea of equality then becomes an ideological desire to mould human kind in a certain direction.[13]

Parekh particularly accuses liberalism of this kind of monistic reasoning. Yet once human nature and individual liberty are dismissed as ideological constructions, it seems as if we are left with the obligation of equally respecting all cultures, and religions, because there is by definition no way of judging between them. When, though, we are confronted with diversity, why should we not simply judge them in our own terms, if that makes us more comfortable? The point of talking about human nature, and our common world, is to remind us that we are part of a wider context, against which our own ideas, and our own culture, must always be set. The fact that human nature transcends all cultures means that there are different ways of meeting its needs. A corollary is that some will be found to be better than others. Once, though, culture is given priority, we are cut loose from any common base. There is nothing in virtue of which I, or others, may be mistaken. Why then should I even respect the right of others to live differently?

THE EQUALITY OF CULTURES?

Multiculturalism pursues the idea of the equality of cultures, but has to do so by removing the possibility of understanding other cultures or seeing value in them. There is nothing with which to judge them or to compare them with our own. Once our culture defines the world for us, there is no incentive to look further. The idea that there are riches to be gained through further understanding from other cultures depends on the idea that they are interpreting the same reality which faces us. No one culture, it may be thought, is likely to possess the whole truth, and we may learn from each other. The uncomfortable consequence, which is fiercely resisted in many quarters, is that just as we may see good in other cultures, some will also be revealed as harmful to human beings, and based on mistaken views. Yet the alternative is to make each culture, however identified, the ultimate arbiter of truth. In an age when more is being regularly revealed, through the human genome programme, of the genetic basis of much human nature, that is a paradoxical position to take.

Multiculturalism can reach the stage of valuing cultures without regard for their content. When a culture, and more specifically a religion, wants to restrict the freedom of its members, the question of how far it can be tolerated becomes a major issue. Positively affirming and 'recognizing' it, as the multiculturalist may want to do, is even more difficult. Yet even referring to 'religion' and 'culture' is to see individuals primarily as members of groups. In addition to the perennial difficulty in defining religion, the thought that any such definition must be culturally biased is already a reflection of the multiculturalist idea that we are each trapped in our culture, and unable to escape its bias.

The fear of prejudice forms a major motive in talking of 'religion or belief' in legal contexts. Any belief, including the denial of all religion, can then be given the protection given to religion. What started with a stress on cultural influence becomes a stress on the rights of individuals, since beliefs can be a personal matter. Unlike a religion, they need not play any cultural role. A belief held by only one person is perfectly possible, while a religion with only one believer is decidedly strange. The association of religion with culture assumes an essential social dimension. Because religions are held collectively, there are restrictions on what can count as following a particular religion. There is normally a distinction between orthodoxy and heresy.

The European Court of Human Rights has drawn back from too great a stress on the individual's point of view. It has made it clear that not everything can count in its eyes as a belief in the relevant sense. Someone may hold a strong opinion or conviction, but that is not enough. This was illustrated in a case brought by a British woman, suffering from motor neurone disease, against the refusal of English law to allow her assistance in committing suicide.[14] As she was paralysed, she was unable to do anything on her own. The Court said that it did not 'doubt the firmness of the applicant's views concerning assisted suicide, but would observe that not all opinions or convictions constitute beliefs in the sense protected by Article 9:1 of the Convention'.

It further restricted the idea of religious freedom when it went on to comment on the issue of freedom to manifest one's religion or belief. It said firmly that 'the term "practice" does not cover each act which is motivated or influenced by a religion or belief.' It thus refused to accept that the mere fact that the applicant believed in personal autonomy meant that she could be free to obtain assistance in killing herself.

The very vagueness of the idea of 'religion or belief' undoubtedly encourages the European Court to define religious practice very narrowly. Even if you are free to believe what you like, the reasoning may go, you cannot be free to put it into practice as you wish. Even strongly held moral beliefs, which result from religious conviction, may not be protected. People can be forced to act against their conscience, even when their conscientious belief is inseparable from wider religious views. The danger is that 'freedom' is restricted to the private realm, and that Article 9 cannot be relied on to guarantee the right to behave in public as one's religion might prompt. At this point, issues both about individual conscience and wider cultural and religious beliefs get consigned to a category of the 'private', over against the public sphere.

This was all made clear in a case about French pharmacists who refused to sell contraceptive pills because of their religious convictions.[15] Just because they were inspired by their religious belief did not mean, according to the European Court, that they could be free to 'manifest their beliefs in a professional sphere'. Given the public stance of '*laïcité*' in France, it is not surprising that the pharmacists were convicted in French courts. It is perhaps more surprising that the European Court should interpret freedom of religion so narrowly as to force people to act against deeply held religious beliefs, even when in a 'public' rather than a 'private' capacity. The question is forcibly raised as to who is to decide what a proper manifestation of religious belief is. If it is the individual, then anything goes. If it is to be the courts, they may be reluctant to become involved in theological judgements about what is a necessary part of belief, and what is separable from it. On the other hand, if the courts stand outside all religion in some 'public space' they may fairly incur the wrath of multiculturalists, among others. They seem to be imposing alien standards on the practice of religion.

Yet as Article 18 of the United Nations Declaration makes clear, freedom of manifestation of religion or belief means freedom 'either alone or in community with others and in public or private'.[16] There does not seem much room for allowing 'private' manifestations and not 'public' ones, if that is the only ground for the distinction. Yet the European Court is quite right in thinking that there must be limits in what counts as religion and religious practice. If autonomous individuals are free to count anything as their religion, or to act as they choose because of their beliefs, the idea of religion loses any meaning. This applies both to individuals and to cultures. Neither can make definitions for themselves in a self-serving way. The multiculturalist might resist classifications made on a basis external to the religion. That, however, rules out nothing.

DISCRIMINATION BETWEEN RELIGIONS

We have already referred to prisoners who attempted to obtain special privileges by pretending they were demanded by religion. Prisons always pose difficult questions about religious liberty, because by definition, prisoners have to be subject to discipline. Most countries provide official chaplains, even of different religions, to help prisoners. Religious liberty is precious even in prison. Yet the authorities have to make decisions about which religious practices are allowable. Some could undermine prison discipline. In the United States, the religious liberty of people in institutions was protected by Section 3 of an Act of the U.S. Congress, the *Religious Land Use and Institutionalized Persons Act* of 2000 (RLUIPA). The complex issues involved reached the Supreme Court in 2005. The balance of powers between State and federal governments became an issue, as did the question whether any special treatment for religion was not tantamount to 'establishment' of religion. Just how sensitive the latter issue can be is illustrated by one American writer on the wider context of law and religion. He says 'The problem of defining religion seems impossible under the Establishment Clause, since any definition would constitute an 'establishment'.[17] That kind of view would lead directly to multiculturalism. If the State cannot give official backing to any distinction between acceptable and unacceptable 'religion', no judgements can be made at all. Yet that means that the State itself can stand for nothing, not even the value of liberty.

In the context of a prison, the character of the religion being espoused has to be taken into account. A prison inmate in Ohio brought claims against prison officials who did not allow facilities for him to practise his religion. He espoused 'Satanism', described to the Supreme Court in his brief as a religion that 'emerged as a protest against Judaeo-Christian spiritual hegemony'.[18] Other plaintiffs were members of the 'Wiccan' religion, apparently related to pre-Christian 'nature religions', members of the 'Asatric' religion, supposedly an ancient polytheistic religion, and members of the 'Christian Identity Church', a small, but avowedly racist, body. How far the plaintiffs were genuine adherents of any such organizations might well be asked, but even if they were, and even if the organizations were to be accepted as bona fide religions, there is still the question whether they should be given special protection by law in prison.

The multiculturalist would demand equal treatment for all religions, without any discrimination. Yet this could provide protection for any activity. The general problem is further illustrated by the fact that when a ban on fox-hunting was being proposed in England in 2004, (and introduced in 2005) some supporters of hunting formed what they termed the 'Free Church of Country Sports' intended to further 'appreciation of our Creator through our activities in the countryside' with special reference to Saint Hubert, the patron saint of hunters.[19] The question, which would have to be settled in the courts, is whether this religious identity (which could be spurious) can give legal protection for the practice of fox-hunting, through an appeal to human rights. Even the possibility that it might illustrates how a claim to 'religion' can provide a means of defying decisions made democratically by legislatures. Unless some content is given in law to the notion of 'religion', religious liberty comes to mean nothing more than the general rights to freedom of thought and conscience which are already protected by charters of human rights, without reference to religion.

In the case of prisons, the U.S. Supreme Court upheld the constitutionality of protecting religious freedom in state-run institutions such as prisons in a way that ruled out picking and choosing between religions. The Court noted that the RLUIPA 'confers no privileged status on any particular religious sect, and singles out no bona fide faith for disadvantageous treatment'.[20] On the other hand, religion should not be allowed to 'trump' the maintenance of order and safety. The Court says that 'we have no cause to believe that RLUIPA would not be applied in an appropriately balanced way, with particular sensitivity to safety concerns'.[21] It reiterates that 'prison security is a compelling state interest'. In particular, racist activity could not be allowed because it would imperil prison security and order.

The Court, however, was not going to rule on the appropriateness of the content of any belief. The only relevant issue is 'the sincerity of a prisoner's professed religiosity'. The opinion of the Court re-iterates a view first expressed by the U.S. Supreme Court in 1965 that 'the "truth" of a belief is not open to question: rather the question is whether the objector's beliefs are "truly held" '.[22] This brings the issue back to the individual. This is an understandable line for the Court to take in a democratic society, which is trying to protect the rights of minorities, even unpopular ones. The task of the law is to preserve freedom, not teach truth. As, however, a maxim, for living together, or for the conduct of public debate, it is a more dubious policy. People's right to hold beliefs must be upheld, but even then there are limits. We cannot, however, in a spirit of easy 'tolerance' and 'respect' think that sincerity is enough. A harmful, and false, belief may be all the more dangerous if sincerely held. Nazis could be sincere. The problem with making the sincerity of an individual the touch-stone of what is publicly acceptable is the same as the basic flaw of multiculturalism. Both dismiss ideas of reason and objective truth. Both resist the idea that there can be informed, rational discussion at a public level, and decisions made in the interests of everyone.

6

The Role of the State

THE SUPREMACY OF GOD?

THE VARIETY of beliefs held by the citizens of a modern democracy will cause problems for any State. Christian schism over the centuries has not helped, but in recent years immigration to many European countries has meant that, for example, there are sizeable Muslim populations in some of them, such as France. This produces a dilemma. If countries endorse any particular set of beliefs, such as the traditional Christian beliefs of the nation, they may alienate sections of the population they wish to integrate. On the other hand, by espousing no beliefs at all, they then set no standards, and have no principles through which the country can be organized. This connects with the problems concerning multiculturalism.

Religion is usually at the centre of these difficulties. A shared religious outlook might help to build up a community, but modern States are built on the principle of religious liberty. We are not, it is thought, automatically born into a religious heritage, and individuals must make their own choices. Indeed it could be argued that there is a religious inheritance which itself stresses the importance of individual commitment. Protestant countries provide an example of this, and in such countries ideals of individual autonomy often clash with the need to pass on the religious understanding which grounds that belief in freedom. Education will always be at the heart of such problems.

The idea of passing on shared values becomes difficult in a State in which there are many religions. Significant opposition to religion, or indifference to it, will also complicate matters. Yet at the same time, any nation, with some system of government, cannot see itself as a haphazard group of people who happen by chance to be in the same place at the same time. They must have a common loyalty to the country and its institutions. A crowd scurrying in different directions across an airport concourse, to travel to different continents, may have in common their common humanity, and that is not a trivial point. They may share little else, whether race, language, religion, or any shared tradition. Some pluralist democracies may seem in danger of becoming like that. Yet the very fact that the bustling airport crowd may have no shared loyalty shows that the freest of democracies cannot allow such disintegration.

The survival of any democracy depends on the character of its citizens. They must respect each other, and be willing to resolve disagreements by democratic means, and not bombs. Yet character cannot be taken for granted. Aristotle saw that virtuous character was produced through learning good habits. Democracy can so encourage individual freedom at the expense of any desire for the common good that it nourishes a destructive egoism. A country composed of those who are only concerned for their own interests may find that its citizens have no loyalty to itself. They may even have no understanding of the importance of the rule of law. These are not just philosophical conundrums but practical problems. Any democracy has to encourage a sense of identity with the wider whole if it is to survive. Any society, which is 'pluralist' but bound together with a single framework of laws, and a common educational system, has to decide what it is to stand for and have taught. No democracy can be wholly neutral about everything, and no pluralist society can simply accept the fact of diversity. Democracies have to preach the virtues of democracy. Pluralist societies have to talk of the importance of tolerance. A nation composed of different communities, whether religious or otherwise, must actively try to encourage the equal acceptance of them all. At this stage, dilemmas multiply. Equal acceptance may seem to imply the neutrality of the State towards all beliefs. Yet the State itself still has to stand for something. A wish to embrace tolerance and diversity may lead it to resist what it sees as religious dogmatism. Yet distancing itself from religion may, from the religious point of view, seem not so very different from outright opposition.

A profound change has occurred in many States if all religious bodies are seen only as voluntary associations to be tolerated and legally protected by the State, but otherwise left alone. Many States have been deliberately identified with a particular religious outlook, even if in countries such as England there is also great toleration of alternative views. The argument is that this could create problems for citizens who reject the official position, and could even constitute opp- ression of minorities. This can happen, when loyalty to a State and membership of a particular religion are identified, but there is another side to the issue. A State that officially recognizes the role of religion, and therefore the existence of God, puts itself under a higher authority. The significance of the phrase in the American Pledge of Allegiance 'one nation under God' is that the State officially says that it is not the final authority, but that its own authority rests on a higher one and has to be judged against that. The Preamble to the Canadian *Charter of Rights and Freedoms* refers to 'the supremacy of God', and this appears to make a similar acknowledgement.[1] As we shall see later, both phrases are challenged, or dismissed as carrying no real claim.

The admission that there is a greater power than the State, and that the State has to be judged by external standards, is momentous. It limits the power of secular authority, if only by insisting that it has to operate according to principles of justice. The entrenchment of rights in constitutions aims to provide a non-religious method of checking power. Yet appeals to rights are insecure in so far as their own status is unclear. They have to be seen as part of a moral order which transcends political agreements, and which may itself be religious in origin, to be effective.

RELIGIOUS HEGEMONY?

According to the political philosopher, John Rawls, political liberalism leaves spiritual questions to the individual, but that is not because it considers them unimportant. He continues: 'This is not to say that religion is somehow "privatized": instead it is not "politicized" (that is, perverted and diminished for ideological ends).'[2] This is certainly a perennial danger, but the reverse is more striking. A liberal State that stands apart from religion, thinking it is a purely individual matter, is saying that politics must be entirely independent of religion, and that religious principles have nothing to say to the real world of political action. Treating religion as just another form of voluntary association, such as a football club, leaves the official workings of the State explicitly and officially distant from any religious principle. States cannot see themselves as under the judgement of God, let alone be called to account because they ignore basic religious principles. Any idea that the authority of the State, like all authority, derives from God, will be dismissed as alien to modern democratic principles. Yet that means that there will be a problem why the organs of the State should be respected, and control the lives of its citizens.

Rawls is opposed to any alignment of State or constitution with any religious viewpoint. He says that 'we must each give up forever the hope of changing the constitution so as to establish a religious hegemony'.[3] In his eyes, that is inconsistent 'with the idea of equal basic liberties for all free and equal citizens'. This follows from the basic idea (linked to his picture of a 'veil of ignorance'[4]) that all political decisions about justices should be taken without regard to how they would affect us. We may want a 'religious hegemony', but what would it be like to live in a society without sharing in the majority faith? Much depends on what is meant by hegemony.

No-one would want to be forced to conform to a religious orthodoxy they rejected. We should not exploit our position as part of the majority to restrict the religious freedom of a minority, because we would ourselves not want to be treated like that if we were in the minority. It is not just that it is wrong to prescribe for others what we would not be willing to suffer ourselves. There is also the practical point that majorities can become minorities over time. By championing freedom for others, one could well be ensuring freedom for oneself at a future time. The Protestant majority in Northern Ireland, for example, cannot be sure that they will always be in the majority.

'Hegemony' need not entail persecution or coercion. Liberals often object to the public recognition of one religion and not another. Yet since it is difficult to relate to religion in general, any society which wants to acknowledge a religious basis, or an authority beyond itself, is inevitably going to favour a particular religion. A general reference to 'God' may be as inclusive as is possible. The problem is that this implies a preference for a religious world-view. It implies a wish for religious principles to apply in a society, even if there is the freedom to reject them. This could suggest hegemony in some form, in that a society is expressing a wish for religion to dominate. That will be rejected by atheists and even by religious people who see religion as so private that it has no relevance for society as a whole.

This watered down version of hegemony involves simply the issue of whether a society as a whole acknowledges God. If it allows total religious freedom, it is likely to be acceptable to a wide range of citizens. To revert to Rawls' 'veil of ignorance', I might object to such public recognition if I think I might be an atheist, but be willing to accept it given the variety of religious beliefs I could possess. This suggests the issue is not pluralism, but the divide between a religious and an explicitly secular way of looking at the world. The apparent liberal solution is to side with the secular against the religious. It may seem like neutrality, but it becomes a much more substantial position, dedicated to divorcing religion from any official context. The pretext is the alleged divisiveness of religion. The result appears to many to be a determined opposition to any public religious expression, and that itself sets up great tensions in a society.

'LA LAÏCITÉ'

France has led the way in separating religion from the public sphere, by upholding a policy of what it terms *'laïcité'*. *'La laïcité'* is a difficult term to translate since it has gained its meaning through its position in French law and society. It upholds absolute neutrality on the part of the organs of the State towards all religion. Since the separation of Church and State in 1905, there has been no question of France being defined as a Catholic nation. The distinction is upheld between the private practice of religion, and a public policy of keeping a distance from it. The State does not support religion, although chaplaincies in hospitals, prisons, and the armed forces have been put in place to facilitate religious freedom.[5] It might look as if 'secularism' is a good translation of *'laïcité'*, and the term is often used. That is, however, usually seen as a sociological term describing social trends, and in particular social disengagement from Church influence. *'La laïcité'* is much more a doctrine, although it should be distinguished from 'laicism', which is a specific anti-religious philosophy.[6] The point of *'laïcité'* is to be neither religious nor anti-religious, since it merely concerns the separation of the official apparatus of the state from any involvement with religion. That prevents State interference with religion just as much as it keeps religion at arms length from government.

France's domestic policy also has its influence on the development of constitutional structures in the European Union. In particular it had a direct influence on the treatment of religion in the proposed European Constitutional Treaty of 2004. One of the many points of controversy was whether the Constitution should make any reference to God, or to Europe's Christian

heritage. Roman Catholic countries such as Poland were insist-
ent that it should, and Pope John Paul supported attempts to
make reference to Europe's Christian roots, and their influence
on Europe's culture and beliefs. Papal support was probably
counter-productive, because many in Europe did not want any
suggestion that somehow power was to be shared with the
Roman Catholic Church. As so often in Europe and the United
States, a latent anti-Catholicism clouds broader debates.
Indeed, the term '*laïcité*' itself clearly involves some contrast
with priestly power. In the end, the relevant clause of the draft
Constitution read:

Drawing inspiration from the cultural, religious and humanist inheritance of Europe, from which have developed the universal values of
the inviolable and inalienable rights of the human person, freedom,
democracy, equality and the rule of law...

Despite a nod in the direction of religious roots, the proposed Constitution made it clear that this is only one of several
sources for 'values' that apparently stand alone, even though
they are 'universal, as well as inviolable and inalienable'.
Anyone who considered the religious foundations of equality,
freedom, and the rule of law as essential would not be satisfied
with the formulation. Those who saw the European Union as
totally secular won the argument. Indeed, France would never
have agreed to anything that did not reinforce the separation of
religion and society. It is perhaps ironic that the French elect-
orate still rejected the Constitution in the referendum of 2005.

At the same time that arguments took place about the
European Union, there were considerable discussions within
France about the domestic import of '*laïcité*'. The presence of a
Muslim population of about five million made such issues even

more pressing. President Chirac had set up an independent commission in 2003 on the issue of religion and the State.[7] In his letter inaugurating the Commission, the President made it clear that '*laïcité*' was a basic element of the French Constitution, the fruit of a long, historical tradition.[8] The first article of the 1946 Constitution, affirmed again in 1958 at the beginning of the fifth Republic, claimed: '*La France est une republique indivisible, laique, democratique et sociale.*'[9] The meaning of its 'indivisible', 'democratic', and 'social' characteristics may be fairly clear, at least at first sight, but '*laique*' is more opaque. Even so, in the words of the Commission, '*la laïcité* ' 'has been placed at the highest level in the hierarchy of norms'.[10] It is intended to encapsulate three values, which are regarded as interlocked and inseparable: freedom of conscience; equality in law for different religious and spiritual choices; and official, political neutrality.[11]

The Commission's view is that '*laïcité*' 'is a means of making individuals coexist who do not share in the same convictions'. Behind this, as President Chirac makes clear, there is a belief that 'the Republic is composed of citizens: it cannot be segmented in communities'.[12] This implies a rejection of multiculturalism, because the Republic has to call on the loyalty of its citizens regardless of their religious beliefs. Something has to transcend the divisive forces that could pull a society apart, as a force for integration. French tradition, dating even from the French Revolution in 1789, has been reluctant to give religion that role.

When the President refers to citizens in contrast to communities, he sounds very individualist. That may apply to the French guarantee of freedom of conscience and of worship. Yet '*la laïcité*' is not an individualist principle, but a communal standard, enforced through public institutions. The meeting-point for citizens of different backgrounds in the public square has to be free itself of all religion. 'Neutrality' becomes a positive demand, requiring, for example, a total lack of discrimination on grounds of religion. From the public standpoint, religion does not usually exist.

Whilst the neutrality of the State entails that no privileges be given to any religious belief, the Commission insists that '*l'État laïque*' (the 'secular' State) should promote neither atheism nor agnosticism. The problem is whether a public space can be neutral, when it has been cleared of all religious influence. Certainly the message is being transmitted by the organs of State that religion is a completely optional, and dispensable, part of human life. As always, education is the area where many battles are concentrated. The more determinedly secular schools become in many countries, in an effort to integrate a diverse population, the more pressure mounts for different religions to have their own schools. In France, the principle of '*laïcité*' often proves incompatible with a dedication to individual freedom of religion. Parents have to have freedom to choose how to bring up their children, and, as a result, they may choose to send them to Catholic schools. Liberals find this galling, and worry about the autonomy of children being infringed through 'indoctrination'. Yet the basic principle is whether parents or the State should control education. As we have seen in the case of the Amish, this is not a straightforward issue. Even so, there is a real danger when the State's understanding of the interests of children drives the process. In the present case, the issue is whether education is better infused with a secular understanding rather than a religious one. The use of State power to enforce its own vision would be an exercise in mere coercion.

The French Commission admits in one comment that 'some Muslim parents already prefer to resort to Catholic schools in order that their children benefit from a teaching of religious values'.[13] This phenomenon has also been remarked on in England, where Muslim parents have chosen religious schools, whether Catholic or Anglican, for the same reason. Religious pluralism seems less worrying for many parents than the stark choice between a religious and a non-religious environment. For believers, whatever motivates the policy, the enforced absence of religion is still an absence.

The Commission also remarks that France is the only European country to have explicitly 'consecrated' *(consacré)* the principle of '*la laïcité*' in its Constitution.[14] The use of the term 'consecrated' in such a context is curious given its religious implications. Indeed there may be a whiff of something like a secular religion here. Certainly after the French Revolution, churches were converted into 'Temples of Reason', and echoes of that atheist tradition may live on. The Commission contrasts the secularization, which now marks Europe (and it uses the word '*secularisation*'), with the situation in the United States 'where religion deeply impregnates society'.[15] This may be a sociological comment, but, as we shall see, there are efforts in the United States to turn the constitutional separation of Church and State into the precise separation of religion from public life, which is characterized by '*laïcité*'.

Only in 1905 did it become clear that the Roman Catholic Church was merely one institution, and certainly not the main one, within the State. The State was the supreme authority. Religious freedom was recognized, but the implication was that it was the prerogative of the State to give that recognition. The corollary is, that despite rhetoric about rights, the State could limit it if it considered it expedient. The French Revolution had marked a sharp change from the idea that society depended for its authority on God, as represented by the Church. Religion was no longer the foundation of the social order. One problem was that relating a society to God in practice led to the will of God being mediated and interpreted by an apparently human institution. That meant that any legitimation provided by such an appeal could easily become perverted into human power politics, so that the hierarchy of the Church tried to dominate society. A reaction to that could lead to a repudiation of all religious belief, or an attempt to keep it within bounds away from the ability to influence politics. '*Laïcité*' does the latter.

THE STATE AS SUPREME

What has sometimes been termed the 'disenchantment' of the world has meant that society was no longer seen as resting on any sacred foundation. This view took root in the later Enlightenment, and was particularly influential in eighteenth-century France. The classic Christian view has been that all authority is transmitted downwards through the sovereignty of God over the political process. St Paul has often been quoted in this context when he says in his letter to the Romans that 'there is no authority but by act of God, and the existing authorities are instituted by Him'.[16] The Enlightenment view was, in contrast, of authority being transmitted upwards by the agreement of the people, perhaps as dramatized in a mythical social contract. The social world need no longer be thought of as dependent on a transcendent order. Instead it is a totally human construction, dependent on nothing beyond itself. This is in many ways a commonplace of social science. Yet if that is the way it is constructed, there could be a certain arbitrariness about its nature. Why should a society be this way rather than that? What legitimates the social order? A religious foundation might sometimes give a spurious legitimation to an unsavoury regime. Without any legitimation, however, instability is imported into the political process, just as relativism beckons on the intellectual front.

The democratic appeal is to the will of the people. Yet that can mean everything depends on the character of citizens, the kind of agreements they make, and the sincerity with which they try to keep them. What forms that character? The refusal to look to any morality or religion as the context in which the people's will should be exercised leaves a dangerous vacuum. The celebration of democracy itself presupposes a belief in the importance of individual humans, and a confidence that they have the freedom and rationality with which to exercise an informed judgement. These presuppositions of democracy have themselves to be given a proper grounding. No State leaves it to chance which 'values' are imbued by children. The term 'values' is itself symptomatic of the more general problem. There is a reluctance to impose 'standards' or to teach 'principles'. 'Values' appear more subjective, and the result of individual choice. Yet in reality, some issues cannot be left to chance, nor to individual choice, if any society is to continue functioning at all, let alone as a cohesive whole. Whatever the rhetoric about personal freedom and individual choice, any public educational system has to ensure that certain 'values' are actually taught.

The French Presidential Commission on '*laïcité*' says firmly: '*L'État a pour vocation de consolider les valeurs communes qui fondent le lien social dans notre pays.*[17] ('The State has a duty to consolidate the communal values which form the basis of social bonding in our country.') An individualist system of values becomes a contradiction in terms, when seen in the context of a nation. Something has to hold it together. Private choice may be defended, but in the end the nation has to be seen, it appears, as itself a community demanding loyalty, and deciding what is and what is not permissible. This is why a break-up into separate communities, on the multiculturalist model, is so deplored in France.

What would be regarded as the necessary restriction of religion, was shown particularly in the banning of 'ostensible' religious apparel from France's classrooms in 2004. Approved overwhelmingly by the French Senate and Chamber of Deputies, this was widely seen as a restriction in particular of the wearing of head-scarves by Muslim girls. We have already seen how this has caused problems in countries as different as Turkey and England. To be even-handed, France also banned other manifestations of religious commitment, such as large crosses. There was concern at external pressure being put on Muslim girls. There was also the desire, in accord with '*laïcité*' that there should be no parading of differences between children of diverse backgrounds. The aim was integration of equal citizens in a united country, and the demands of the State were primary.

The argument of the Commission was that the individual citizen benefits through the policy surrounding '*laïcité*', by the protection of freedom of conscience.[18] In return, they say, 'a public space has to be respected in which all can participate'. The starting-point, it seems, is not individual freedom. If it were, it could not be part of a trade-off between private and public. Schools have to be neutral and on their guard against aggressive proselytizing. There has to be 'this equilibrium between rights and duties'.[19] Rights, it seems, must be balanced against the needs of the State, and the loyalty it requires.

The insistence of a State that it regulate and control the public influence of religion shows how religion can be placed in a subordinate role. It is tolerated, but it has to know its place, and that place has to be rigidly defined by the relevant secular authorities. It has been said that '*laïcité*' 'carries with it the right for religion to exist without being dominated by the state'.[20] There is no governmental interference in the internal affairs of a religion or denomination. But the role of religion is pre-determined by the State. It is kept out of State schools, and '*l'école laique*' (the 'secular' school) has been called the 'fundamental institution of *la laïcité*'.[21] That is because the school is typically seen as an engine of social integration. The school, the Commission asserts, must be a neutral space ('*un éspace de neutralité*').[22]

In all this, there is the paradox that to recognize diversity, there first has to be unity. For there to be freedom of religion, it appears there has to be a sense of loyalty to a State which is independent of religion. For there to be individual choice, there has to be social cohesion, reinforced by a State system of education. In the case of the head-scarf, the French State was placing the equality of the sexes before any idea of religious freedom. Whether one agrees or not in that particular case, the values of the State are in conflict with religious obligations and in such a case the State wins.

Many countries face this tug between a respect for diversity and the needs of national unity. France has gone further than most in making a doctrine about the separation of religion and

State into a positive principle, to be taught and enforced in a way which is seen as maintaining national identity. In any tug between individual and State, the State is always going to use its power to define the terms of the argument. France is reluctant to accept the existence of religious communities as intermediaries such is its fear of the consequences of multiculturalism.

Once a State repudiates any religious foundation for itself, it recognizes no check on its powers beyond those it is prepared to recognize. It can control the public sphere, and indeed count it a virtue that no religious agenda can intrude. The more it is accepted that character can be formed by communities within the State, and that citizens can look to religious authorities for guidance, the less any government can be confident of its ability to set its own standards. The ultimate loyalties of citizens will have been formed in a non-religious context. Yet religious liberty is such a basic element of freedom that only a totalitarian State will dare restrict it significantly. This then creates its own momentum within any society. For example, the more secular a school system becomes, the more pressure there will be for confessional schools. This produces a splintering of the public educational system, and the very division into communities which the French in particular wish to avoid.

A search for national cohesion in the face of religious diversity can result in the imposition of a secular world-view which challenges the religious commitment of individuals. Religious freedom can never be absolute, becoming a cloak for damaging and harmful practices. At the same time, there should always be a presumption of its importance. When a State as a matter of policy intends to further its own interests by setting limits to the role of religion, it is setting itself up as a higher authority than any religion. When the Presidential Commission in France talked of a school providing a 'neutral space', it also upheld it as 'a place of the awaking of the critical conscience'.[23] Neutrality and rationality may go together but that is a large assumption. There seems to be an implication that freeing the schools of any religious influence helps the flourishing of a critical conscience. It is thus the absence of religion, and not its presence, which encourages critical reflection. Rationality, it seems, implies a distancing from religious authority. This is a typical Enlightenment view, opposing reason to religion, and critical thinking to tradition. So far from constituting neutrality, it merely exemplifies a particular current in European thought.

CUSTOM AND LIBERTY

The continuing ambiguity about the place of diversity and of freedom is the level at which they should operate. When diversity is extolled, is it a diversity of individual belief, or a diversity of belief-systems? Multiculturalism stresses the latter, while liberals concentrate on the former. Similarly while individual choice is stressed, stress can also be given to the need to understand and respect different religions as bodies of belief. There is a constant oscillation between the individual and wider tradition. John Stuart Mill in his essay 'On Liberty' was in no doubt that individual freedom mattered, rather than the dead-weight of 'custom'. He talks of the despotism of 'custom' as 'everywhere the standing hindrance to human advancement'.[24] With a touching nineteenth-century faith in progress and 'improvement', he said that only liberty could be their unfailing source, 'since by it there are as many possible centres of improvement as there are individuals'. Yet there is a paradox in this, since, even in science, each generation depends on what went on before. Belief systems, including religions, cannot be continuously reinvented. Science needs its traditions, and they presuppose the existence of an ongoing community.

Education is often the lynch-pin, and Mill himself saw its importance in the maintenance of liberty. For this reason he opposed education being in the hands of the State. He would not have been surprised at the ideological overtones in French education. He said that 'a general State education is a mere contrivance for moulding people to be exactly like one another'. He adds that the mould is whatever happens to please the 'predominant power' in the government of the time. He believed in individuality of character and diversity of opinions, and so advocated 'diversity of education'. The problem is that education cannot but presuppose traditions, customs, and beliefs, or otherwise there is little to teach. They may not replace individual choice but they have to precede and inform it.

The more that individual liberty, and rights of choice of education, are upheld, the more it is tacitly assumed that we all need to be introduced to traditions of thought and belief. Without any tradition, liberty becomes meaningless. We do not know what we are choosing. There may be an issue of which traditions we should be first taught, since we cannot learn everything at once. Liberals fear that teaching any particular tradition is a form of despotism, to use Mill's term, or indoctrination. They rarely say this about science, but they may well do about religion. As a result they would advocate State education in common schools and bitterly oppose specific religious schools, for different denominations, and even for different religions.

In the United States, Churches and other religious bodies have their own educational programmes, apart from the general educational system. There is, however, the danger that this makes for religion being marginalized. Its teaching can be made to seem irrelevant to the central concerns of public schools and universities, and may even be contradicted by them, without any attempt at the rational comparison of different possibilities. Even so, a free society cannot make everyone go to 'common schools' without an unacceptable degree of compulsion. Even France recognizes that. Precisely, therefore, because of a concern for individual liberty, religious schools have to be tolerated, and perhaps even encouraged. If State support is not forthcoming, like-minded parents will pool resources to form schools which can reflect the beliefs of the parents.

There is thus the continual oscillation between individual and community. The more that individual freedom is exercised, the more institutions will be formed and perpetuated to transmit particular beliefs and traditions. The choice between liberty and the constraints of tradition is a false one. Indeed, as Mill implies, the more that public education is designed to encourage total liberty, the more it is probably itself being driven by the social agenda of the government. Freedom cannot operate in a vacuum, and in the absence of traditional forms of guidance, those with the power will exert their influence.

Some liberals come near to suggesting that the constraint of truth is an unacceptable assault on liberty. That is why diversity sometimes seems a proof of liberty. Yet this cannot be an individual matter, since it needs the existence of ongoing institutions and traditions of belief to provide the material from which choices can be made. Such institutions, to be effective, need to have a public character, and to exist within a recognized public framework. It is not surprising that there is so much pressure in many countries for religious schools. The less public recognition of religion there is, the more agitation there will be for a compensating public presence for institutions which can offer what, in some countries such as France, the State clearly does not.

7

Must Democracy Be Religiously Neutral?

COMMITMENT OR TOLERATION?

A DEMOCRATIC country is one in which government is answerable to the people, and can be dismissed by them in an election. A pre-condition of exercising that democracy is an individual freedom according to which all citizens are free to form judgements about what is important, and to live life accordingly. A State in which citizens are told what to think, or conditioned through lack of information to accept certain things as true, is controlling its citizens rather than being controlled by them. Yet freedom is indivisible. Freedom to choose a government is linked to freedom to choose a religion or reject all religion. I cannot be free in one direction, but be controlled in another. I must either be able to see for myself what is true in every context, or I am not allowed to think for myself.

Religious freedom, however, is not a mere by-product of democracy. Jurgen Habermas puts religious freedom at centre stage when he writes: 'Pluralism and the struggle for religious tolerance were not only driving forces behind the emergence of the democratic state, but continue to stimulate its further evolution up to now.'[1]

As a matter of historical fact, ideas of religious freedom were prominent in the Reformation, and the Enlightenment. It has been an element in many social upheavals in Europe over the last five centuries. The quest for religious freedom was a major force behind immigration to the United States, and not just in its formative years. It is not surprising that, if religion is at the centre of people's lives, a quest for freedom of belief and practice would provide the motive for the acquisition of wider liberties.

The development of law, particularly at the international level, has to take increasing notice of the need to protect religious liberty. In Europe, the European Convention on Human Rights is being invoked more and more. One might expect that all religions would welcome the enforcement of such freedom, but even a freely chosen belief must be constrained by what is true. There is no point in having the belief, if we do not think it true. This raises the possibility of a clash between a desire for freedom and the need to respect truth. How far should error be tolerated? For someone with no religious commitment, it may seem that all religions can be equally tolerated as long as the right to keep clear of all of them is protected. Yet that neglects the fact that from a secular viewpoint some, and even all, religions can be seen as harmful. Must a society tolerate continuing and sustained damage to itself? It all depends on who is defining the damage, just as the concern for truth raises the further question of who, in a society, is going to decide what is true.

The idea of objective truth is central to much religion.[2] Modern attempts to re-interpret religious assertions, so that they do not claim a truth that applies to everyone, attenuate religious belief. Eventually it will appear to claim nothing, with no reason to become committed to it or to remain committed.[3] One motive for philosophical attempts to tone down the exclusive claims of Christianity is a fear of encouraging intolerance towards other religions. Yet Christianity makes specific claims about the nature of the world and God's relation to it. It asserts that in Christ God makes a unique revelation of Himself. As such, it has to contradict other religions which would deny this, even if they honour Jesus. It might appear that if Christianity would only stop making an exclusive claim to truth, we could begin to remove causes of dissension. Apart from the underlying intellectual dishonesty of such an approach, it is doubtful if other religions would reciprocate. Islam, for example, is hardly going to change its claims to truth to suit Christians.

The path to mutual toleration should not lie in giving up beliefs, or, worse, pretending not to believe what we plainly do. Mutual respect can only come through a shared willingness to seek a truth which holds universally, even if we do not fully grasp it at present. It cannot be the result of a political attempt to minimize differences. Religion matters only because truth does. The difficulty is how to hold firmly to one's own religious beliefs while recognizing that others can also have insights into the nature of reality. If we love truth, though, we do it no service by ceasing to abide by our best estimate of where the truth lies.

Religion demands our utmost commitment, but by definition it deals with what goes beyond our understanding. If there is a God, His nature has to surpass the ability of human minds to understand, or human language to describe it. When finite and fallible humans try to lay hold of the character of the infinite, they will fail. Any religion referring to a transcendent God has to explain how God can be understood in human terms. That is the philosophical justification for revelation. Unless God comes down to human level, by, say, speaking through prophets, or being revealed by His Son, the gap between transcendent reality and the human situation will seem unbridgeable.

An absolute commitment to one's religion, as evidenced by complete trust in the God who is the object of one's beliefs, may be essential. Such belief does not guarantee truth. The world has been well populated throughout its history by those who have been certain about many things, and have been wrong. Certainty and sincerity are not enough, Humility, and even humility towards the truth, is also a religious virtue. The difficulty is finding a balance between firm commitment and a respect for truth. Infallibility is not a human characteristic, and others can also have what they see as good reasons for a different set of beliefs.

We are threatened on the one side by relativism, and on the other, by dogmatism born of passionate commitment. If we think that certainty guarantees knowledge, we can quickly slide into a refusal to recognize the right of others to disagree on the grounds that they are just falling into simple error and should be corrected. This oscillation between relativism and dogmatism creates many problems for religion. It can seem that the alternative to religious persecution is to abandon the possibility of any universal and objective truth, which all should ideally recognize. Yet once that happens, so far from religions being windows on reality, they become human traditions, which themselves are as likely to sow discord as heal strife.

Giving up exclusive claims to truth is not the answer, as that would remove a prime reason for belonging to a faith. Once any religion doubts the validity of its own beliefs it is in deep trouble, and must lose confidence it itself. In Christianity, some radical theology has had this effect. Somehow we must accept that different religions do make claims to truth, and they can contradict each other. We have to accept that human freedom, and particularly the freedom to hold and practise a religion, is one of the most precious elements in being human. A willingness to respect other beliefs should not undermine our determination to abide by our own. Yet an absolute commitment to one's own should not lead one to despise the deep commitments of other faiths. In fact we should be able to respect them more. Given our shared human nature, we can recognize that we react in different ways to the same challenges.

TRUTH VERSUS FREEDOM?

Religions have often valued truth more than any estimation of the value of human freedom. The free will, which is an important component in much Christian theology, may itself be the source of much modern democratic thought. Thus truth for a Christian includes the demand that all humans must be free to make their own response to God. There are, however, always currents in religion which are impatient with talk of individual freedom. Their concern for truth, and a consequent willingness to impose it on others takes precedence. The Roman Catholic Church has historically been accused of not respecting religious liberty, but in the contemporary world, it is often Islam which challenges 'Western' ideas of freedom and human rights.

Must Democracy Be Religiously Neutral?

Many Islamic countries have severe punishments for converting to another faith. To take examples, mentioned by two Islamic writers, Saudi Arabia considers conversion to another religion 'apostasy', and such public apostasy is punishable by death[4]. In Sudan, we are told, 'while non-Muslims may convert to Islam, the 1991 Criminal Act makes all apostasy, including conversion to another religion by Muslims, punishable by death'. Yemen adopts a similar policy. The reasoning for such draconian action is that people who have never seen the truth may be treated differently, but those who have been committed to it have no excuse for turning away to falsehood. There is a simple equation between truth and Islam, and fierce dogmatism can give rise to intolerance of any who stray. The position is summed up as follows by the same authors who also point out that changing one's religion is not recognized by Islam as a right. They say:

In line with the arguments advanced by classical Muslim jurists, many Muslims today agree that Islam is the true and final religion, and that turning from this true religion to another which is, by definition, 'false', cannot be tolerated. Since salvation is the most important objective for a human being, all attempts should be made, in their view, to keep the person within the fold of Islam, the only path to salvation.[5]

Views of this kind over the centuries have also encouraged forced conversion to Islam, and Christianity itself has sometimes produced similar attitudes. The difficulty is always the balance between truth and toleration. A writer on the role of the European Court of Human Rights makes the point that 'as with the Catholic church and indeed most religions that claim exclusive access to the truth, religious freedom is valuable in

Islam only to the extent that it can be accommodated within the teachings of the religion'.[6] Her conclusion is:

> In a religiously pluralistic Europe, the Court should thus be wary of drawing too heavily on religious models as a basis for freedom of religion or belief. While some individuals may respect religious freedom because of their religious beliefs, others may have to be forced to respect the freedom of others despite their religion or belief.[7]

The assumption appears to be that the Court must, because of 'pluralism', not identify itself with any religion, but somehow value religious freedom in a religious vacuum. This may seem wise, as a strategy for impartial legal judgement, but religious liberty cannot consistently be upheld in a philosophical vacuum. The same writer stresses that the European Court 'needs to develop a philosophy of freedom of religion or belief that gives emphasis to the autonomy of the individual and the development of a pluralistic and democratic society'.[8] Yet a problem about an emphasis on autonomy is that it can easily degenerate into a subjectivism which decrees that every person's judgement is final, at least for them. Autonomy comes to mean not just freedom from coercion, but the ability to decide what shall be true for each individual. We slip quickly from the innocuous principle that we must all make up our own minds to the view that there are no external standards of truth to which we are all accountable.

Democracy can soon become associated with an extreme individualism, so that, in some matters at least, it will be denied that there are any experts. Democracy is then associated with the kind of pluralism which holds that different beliefs have all to be regarded as equally valid by the State because they have been freely chosen. Truth drops out of the picture, because of the fear of the State backing one version of the truth. Yet being aligned with an unbridled subjectivism is hardly conducive to teaching the importance of democracy. We cannot take it for granted that people will come to see that for themselves. In the name of freedom, we have to be willing to point to at least some truth, which is not the creation of individual judgement. Protecting democracy is not an abuse of authority, since it is intended to further the interests of all individuals. The argument can never simply be about the rights of individuals as against authority. To be implemented, rights depend on the use of authority both in teaching and in enforcement. The question is where the limits of authority should be. Some would argue that the law has a purely procedural role, but the worth of democracy as a system, and the values of freedom and tolerance it encourages, are matters of substance, and should be of concern to the State.

Once democracy becomes aligned with ideals of diversity and autonomy, it can seem at odds with any religious concern for truth. The American political philosopher, Michael Walzer writes, in connection with religious toleration: 'Virtually all the tolerated religions aim to restrict individual freedom'.[9] He adds that 'most religions are organized to control behaviour'. To a liberal, this appears intolerable, but liberalism requires the control of intolerance. Liberals may themselves seek restrictions on religious liberty in the name of a more general freedom. Walzer gives as an example of religious intolerance the way in which, in the United States, 'the more extreme members of religious majorities aim to control everyone's behaviour in the name of a supposedly common (Judaeo-Christian say) tradition of "family values", or of their own certainties of what is right and wrong'.[10]

This description is not entirely fair. Just as liberals have a vision of a free society, encouraging individual autonomy, and resulting in a radical diversity, some adherents of a religion might have an alternative one. This does not arise from their own certainty—a subjectivist way of looking at it—or from a particular tradition, even as wide as the Judaeo-Christian one. That is a quintessentially relativist way of looking at the situation. Christians and others who hold moral views about what constitutes a good society would not see themselves as primarily upholding a tradition, let alone giving rein to their personal preferences. They would see themselves as acting in the name of truth, and advocating policies which are right and beneficial for everyone, whatever their beliefs. To a liberal it can seem monstrous that appeals should be made to 'truth' rather than individual choice. The argument is illustrated by fierce battles in the United States about abortion, between those who champion individual liberty, and the right to a free choice, and those who appeal to alleged truths about human life. Different ideas of what is right are at issue. Even liberals want others to acquiesce in the view which they regard as right but which their opponents do not. The argument is not about preferences, certainties, or traditions, but about what is morally right, and that means ultimately what is most conducive to human flourishing.[11]

A decision has to be made about what standards a society must adopt, and there will have, at some point, to be a refusal to tolerate those who disagree. The issue is often how far tolerance can extend, not that it is inexhaustible. Those who believe in tolerance cannot tolerate intolerance. No-one can escape arguments about what is true, and sometimes truth needs to be acknowledged as such by everyone. Yet there will still be problems. Enforced liberalism will be as objectionable to some, as dogmatic intolerance is to liberals.

RELIGIOUS AUTHORITY

Questions of truth may appear to be the life-blood of religion. Does that mean that ordinary standards of democracy are inappropriate within religious bodies? The most democratic wings of Protestantism, such as Congregationalism, aided the growth of Western democracy. Even there, however, there is a question of how far basic doctrinal issues can be decided by majority vote. There have to be some standards of belief, if only the Bible itself, for there to be a gospel to preach. The more that the content of belief is left to the conscience of the individual, the more the whole purpose of a Church's existence has to be put in doubt. In the end it could come to stand not for the transmission of any particular faith, or body of belief, but for religious liberty, and the right of each member to decide what to believe. Some will be bound to wonder what is the point of belonging to such an organization.

The plight of the Unitarians is an example. In England, at least, they have almost ceased to exist, after being in the eighteenth century merely a liberal, and intellectual, form of Protestantism, which seceded from the Presbyterian Church. Religious liberty may be a noble creed, but there is little point in preaching it, if there is nothing left to believe in. From being Christ-centred, Unitarianism drifted into a vague and unfocused benevolence to humanity, and became virtually indistinguishable from humanism.

Not surprisingly, most Christian Churches see the dangers of such unbridled freedom, and make the preservation and transmission of doctrine a central feature of their discipline. Some exercise authority without any pretence at democracy. The Roman Catholic Church is the prime example. The Anglican Church's emphasis on the role of bishops as the guardians of doctrine is another example of an emphasis on the role of truth. Other Churches give a greater place to democracy, while also trying to hold to sound doctrine. Thus the Conference of the Methodist Church is elected, but collectively exercises an episcopal oversight. Whatever the method, some form of authority is essential if truth is to be preserved and passed on to future generations. Majority votes, let alone individual decisions, cannot settle truth.

Does this mean that democracy and truth are uneasy bedfellows? The problem lies particularly in the exercise of authority. A particular religion may believe that it possesses truth. As a result, it is reasonable for it to enforce its standards on those who voluntarily wish to adhere to it. In other words, people have willingly submitted to its authority, and wish to accept its teaching. There is little point in belonging to any religion if one's only wish is to repudiate it. The problem comes when, just because a religion believes in an objective truth which applies to everyone, it considers that it has a duty to ensure that adherents cannot reject its authority, and leave. It can believe that others outside should be made to accept the religion through forcible conversion, or at the very least, to abide by the rules of the religion whether they want to or not. That is the reverse of the freedom required for the proper functioning of democracy. The dilemma is how to reject relativism, and yet not fall into the authoritarian approach which makes democratic freedom impossible.

The demands of one community, or collectivity, cannot be extended to apply to the whole society of which that community may only be a part. What happens, though, when a society as a whole is identified with a particular religious outlook? Those who reject the religion may seem to be rejecting the standards of the society of which they are citizens. The argument may not be so much about truth as about identity. Who belongs and who does not? Bitter conflicts occur precisely when religious commitment and issues of national or cultural identity become confused. The problems of Northern Ireland have much to do with appeals to two different historical identities, and the resulting commitments to different brands of Christianity. The situation is even worse when one religion has a monopoly and a refusal to subscribe to it is then seen as treachery to the nation. Religion is a powerful source of cultural identity, and the worst situations occur when religion is seen just as a badge of nationality, or what makes 'us' us, rather than a basic element in the human search for truth. It is not so much the belief in truth that is the culprit, as forgetting that truth is at stake and making religion fulfil a different function.

An Example: Moldova

The attitude of the European Court on Human Rights to religious issues was clarified in a case where issues of identity appeared to loom large.[12] The Republic of Moldova is one of the successor States to the Soviet Union, sandwiched between the Ukraine and Romania. In the whole of Eastern Europe, the collapse of Communism has produced a search for various national identities, and traditional religious allegiances have once again been invoked. In Moldova, with the ebbing of Russian power, and with a significant population of Romanian origin, some have looked to Romania. It was feared that they would press for union, so the future of the new, independent Republic was at stake. The Orthodox Church in Moldova was pulled in two directions, to Romania and to Russia. A breakaway 'Metropolitan Church of Bessarabia' with a million members, looked to the Patriarchate of Bucharest, instead of to Moscow. The Government of Moldova held the power to refuse recognition to the newly constituted Church, and hence to be allowed to function. It did this, saying that it did not infringe freedom of religion as the adherents of the Church could still function as Orthodox Christians. The case was regarded as an administrative one within the Church, though one with alarming political overtones.

On appeal to the European Court, the Court notes that 'in the absence of recognition, the applicant Church may neither organise itself nor operate'.[13] Despite the fears of the Moldovan Government, the Court found no evidence that the express purpose of the Church was any different from that stated in its articles of association. There is the implication that if the Church was clearly seen to be working towards political unification with Romania, that might be a ground for restricting freedom of religion. As the second clause of Article 9 of the European Convention makes clear, there can be limitations on freedom to manifest religion as long as they are necessary in a democratic society.

The Court took the opportunity in its judgement of laying down general principles about religion and democracy. It claims that 'true religious pluralism . . . is inherent in the concept of a democratic society'.[14] Freedom of thought, conscience, and religion forms 'one of the foundations of "a democratic society" within the meaning of the constitution'.[15]

Such freedom helps to make up the identity of believers, but the Court says that 'it is also a precious asset for atheists, agnostics, sceptics and the unconcerned'. Thus freedom of religion includes the freedom to reject it or to be unconcerned with it. These rights have to be protected in a democracy, and the Court accepts that, in a society of different beliefs, some restrictions on freedom may be necessary to ensure that everyone's beliefs are respected. This line of reasoning, however, could suggest that there are dangers in a State aligning itself with one community or any particular set of religious beliefs. According to the Court, in its relations with different religious outlooks, the State 'has a duty to remain neutral and impartial'.[16] What is at stake 'is the preservation of pluralism and the proper functioning of democracy'. Furthermore it argues, 'the autonomous existence of religious communities is indispensable for pluralism in a democratic society'. The right to religious freedom 'excludes assessment by the State of the legitimacy of religious beliefs or the ways in which those beliefs are expressed'.

This clarion call for pluralism as a constituent part of democracy, and for the neutrality and impartiality of the State to religion, may go further than is warranted by the need to protect religious liberty. The idea that the State should not assess the 'legitimacy' of religious beliefs, or their expression, is badly phrased. 'Legitimacy' is precisely what the State is concerned with, since what is legitimate is what is lawful, and the State has to decide how far any individual or group is going against its own laws, perhaps by interfering with the rights of others. Presumably the Court was thinking that the State should not make rational judgements about the truth of different beliefs. It is no function of government to pronounce on how far beliefs are justified, or to determine what its citizens ought to believe.

In a free and democratic society, a government should attempt to reflect the freely chosen views of its citizens, and not try to mould them. Otherwise the government is assuming a knowledge it cannot pretend to. As John Stuart Mill said in 'On Liberty' 'all silencing of discussion is an assumption of infallibility'.[17] He points out: 'complete liberty of contradicting and disposing our opinion is the very condition which justifies us in assuming its truth for purposes of action'.[18] Freedom and rationality can never be prised apart. The exercise of the one demands the other. Those with no freedom cannot decide what is true.

Yet things are not so simple. The European Convention in the second clause of Article 9 assumes that religious expression can be limited because of such factors as public safety and order, health and morals, and the protection of others' rights and freedoms. These will never be self-evident, depending on judgements about what is in the interest of human beings. Their importance itself depends on some prior vision of the world and the place of us all in it. What counts as ordered and safe depends on the kind of society needed. 'Health' and 'morals' are themselves contested concepts, as is witnessed by the willingness of some totalitarian States to categorize forms of religious belief as themselves types of mental disorder. Governments have to stand somewhere to make any decision. The demand that they be neutral between all possible views would reduce them to paralysis. Even the idea that neutrality to all religion 'and belief' can be consistent with a definite moral stance is questionable. It somehow ignores the fact that morality can be as controversial as any religion.

Must Democracy Be Religiously Neutral?

Must a government be morally neutral in a pluralist society? That either means that it does nothing, or that it becomes unscrupulous.

Governments themselves need criteria for what constitutes fair and just practice. If ideas of justice are ultimately derived from ideas about God, or a divinely instituted natural law, the idea that a government must itself be religiously neutral in order to respect religious freedom could be the reverse of the truth. What is necessary is that its laws are impartial and neutral and allow everyone to practise their own religion as they see fit. In the case of Moldova, the Government's distrust of the breakaway Church of Bessarabia, together with a concern for national security, ensured that the Church had no legal status, and could not protect any assets. This meant that its members could not practise their religion. That, though, was an issue that should have been independent of the wider suspicions of the Government of Moldova.

The point of a free society is that people do not have to do what a government wants or sees as desirable. In Moldova, there was no need for the Government to show approval of the breakaway Church, or even, if it so decided, to deal with it on the same basis as other branches of the Orthodox Church. It only had to give citizens the freedom to join it, and the Church the freedom to function. How the Government then related to it was a further matter for political decision. Religious liberty, and the changing attitudes of government must not be inter-dependent, given the rule of law and a proper recognition of the right of religious freedom. The point of legal protection for religion is to insulate it from the political climate at any given time.

The kind of impartiality required by organs of the State is a willingness to have fair laws, applied consistently. Moldova was prepared to administer the law in a way which the European Court found biased. The law was made an instrument of politics. Yet the Court's insistence on governmental neutrality could be interpreted as demanding that the State be itself detached from all identification with religion. The view that pluralism is vital for democracy can be equally ambiguous. Must diversity of belief be positively encouraged, and must a State officially show no preference between belief and unbelief?

A MORAL GOVERNMENT OR A NEUTRAL ONE?

In conditions of less than perfect knowledge, and of fallibility, there will always be disagreement. In a free society, which does not resort to coercion, universal agreement in many areas, including religion, is unlikely. Without enforced conformity, there is, as a result, going to be variation of belief. To avoid the arbitrary imposition of the assumptions of one religion in a misplaced act of power, it may seem that legislators and politicians must remain impartial. The result may be that a Christian government is ruled out, in the sense of one operating through the application of explicitly Christian principles. This raises the question of what principles any government should have. It will be barred from drawing them from any religion. Yet many would argue that there is a connection between morality and more general world-views. Saying that there is none may make it easier to banish religion from the public sphere, but it is already to take a controversial, and substantive position. How we view our fellow human beings, and why we think they matter, seems to depend on wider views of our place in the scheme of things. A government that has to be neutral about all such belief-systems will act in a moral vacuum. Such neutrality is sometimes assumed to be ethically superior to one in which a government aligns itself with a particular religion, but what can that ethical judgement be based on?

Even so, arguments about the need for official neutrality about religion apply in the case of morality as well. If there is no social consensus over what is morally important or desirable, this is an argument for official neutrality about all morality, as much as religion. That, however, is self-evidently absurd unless morality and politics have nothing to do with each other. A government would even have to be neutral about the importance of justice and fairness themselves. There could then be no moral argument for toleration, or freedom, or any compelling moral reason for neutrality.

Any state has to make judgements about what is conducive to the public good. The need for the law to be impartial is itself a basic moral demand. Any government, interested in anything beyond the blind exercise of power, has to have a moral vision, and this has to come from somewhere. The demand for individual freedom is itself a basic moral requirement, and so democracy itself can only flourish in a moral context. So far from democracy requiring pluralism of belief, and official neutrality to different beliefs, it has to be carefully nourished. A morally sterile environment is likely to destroy it.

The mere existence of different views may be the result of freedom. A properly functioning democracy, however, cannot rest content with the proliferation of views, or the fact of competing groups. The European Court itself stressed that a principle characteristic of democracy 'is the possibility it offers of resolving a country's problems through dialogue'.[19]

Democracy does not just spawn disagreement, but provides a mechanism by which citizens can communicate with each other, and find ways of living together. Diversity can only exist against a wider background of mutual tolerance. There have to be wider loyalties than merely to one of the disputing groups.

Pluralism, in the sense of divergent beliefs unwilling to communicate with each other, is a threat to the functioning of democracy. The 'preservation of pluralism' advocated by the European Court cannot be the ultimate aim of any democracy. It could all too easily result in the establishment of self-contained groups refusing mutual dialogue. The problem with the elevation of such 'pluralism' into an essential component of democracy, rather than its by-product, is that the emphasis of differences means that each system becomes locked into its own world. Pluralism becomes relativism, and relativism removes the possibility of a common rationality.

All this applies particularly in religion. The fear of one religion exercising control, or power, over another, may sometimes be real. Democracy, however, needs not the preservation, or celebration, of difference, but the establishment of a common public space, in which rational discussion can take place. Different religions can be respected because they should all be contributing to discussions of the nature of the common good. A society content with the fact of divergent beliefs is already fragmenting. There must be a public space where all voices can be heard, and perhaps agreements achieved.

The paradox is that the establishment of such a common space already depends on a respect for democratic principles, including the idea that each person is equally important, and should be free to make up his or her own mind about religious commitment. That may be the pre-condition of democracy, but it is a morally distinctive position. Some countries (and not just Islamic ones) would vehemently repudiate it. It may be unsettling for some to reflect that some of its roots may have been nourished by Christianity. If that is so, it was religious commitment, not religious neutrality on the part of nations, which produced a framework in which all can be free.

8

Law and Religion

THE CANADIAN CHARTER

A CHRISTMAS tree was being erected at the end of November in front of Toronto's distinctive City Hall. At least it looked like a Christmas tree. It was being erected in time for Advent, or, more likely, the Christmas shopping season. Then a media storm blew up. A city official had decreed that, despite all appearances, it was a 'Holiday' tree. The city authorities were apparently succumbing to the reluctance evident in the United States to refer to Christmas rather than just 'the holidays'. In Toronto, the Mayor stepped in and said the tree was in fact a Christmas tree. He commented that just because people had to respect the traditions of others, it did not mean that they could not celebrate their own.

This apparently trivial incident symbolizes the dilemma facing religion in public life. Is it offensive to other religions to admit the fact of a Christian heritage? Significantly, those who actually belong to other religions rarely complain. In Toronto, the issue was quite literally about a Christian presence in the public square. It was all the more controversial because there was a time when Toronto was quite sure that it was a Christian city, with strict laws about Sunday observance, whereas now, with massive immigration, it could not be more cosmopolitan. The idea that the city was aligning itself with one section of the population may have seemed objectionable. Yet there seemed a whiff of hypocrisy about the affair, since the tree was clearly related to a particular tradition, and changing its name could not disguise the fact.

Canada has had to grapple with more intractable problems than the naming of a tree, but many of them stem from the difficulties of trying to respect diversity, while trying to hold the nation together. Canada's roots lie in combining two European cultures, two languages, and, some would say, two religions. That, though, is to exaggerate differences between Protestantism and Roman Catholicism, both of which would have welcomed the Toronto 'Christmas' tree. One way of meeting with cultural tensions in Canada has been to stress the rights of Canadians in ways that can be protected by the courts. The aim is for the country to be inclusive, tolerating diversity within a wider whole. The project is a precarious one, but the Canadian solution in recent years has been to rely on the *Charter of Rights and Freedoms*, which already serves as a model for similar charters in countries such as South Africa and New Zealand. The *Charter* was part of the Constitution Act of 1982, under which ultimate responsibility for the Canadian Constitution was transferred from Westminster to Ottawa.

The Charter has had a major impact on the treatment of religion in public life. Its clauses are expressed in the widest possible terms. As we saw in Chapter 4, they proclaim equality and outlaw discrimination in Article 15, while also demanding in Article 27 that everything is interpreted 'in a manner consistent with the preservation and enhancement of the multi-cultural heritage of Canadians'.[1] There is scope, given the open-ended nature of such aspirations, for the courts to turn the law in surprising directions. Fine-sounding principles can only be made to apply in concrete situations by the judgement of a Supreme Court, replacing Parliament as the final arbiter. In the case of religion, there is a tendency for questions about religion in public life to be seen particularly in terms of challenges to equality, and the overriding need not to discriminate between one citizen and another. For the law to favour the practices of a particular religion would imply that one set of citizens are valued more than another set.

There is a fear that, in a democratic society, elected representatives will follow the will of the majority, resulting in injustice to minority groups. Should non-Christians be compelled to abide by a legal regime which is avowedly Christian? Should a minority language group be forced to speak the language of the majority? Courts are thought to be better at safeguarding minority rights. The existence of legally enforceable charters of rights do, however, make for a considerable change in understanding the role of Parliament in countries such as Canada and the United Kingdom, used to the traditional doctrine that Parliament is sovereign. Once the European Convention of Human Rights was included in the domestic law of the United Kingdom by the *Human Rights Act* of 1998 it was clear that the decisions of judges will, in practice, impinge more on British life than they have in the past. It will be difficult for the United Kingdom Parliament to ignore judgements that human rights have been violated, even though it retains that right, since the moral force of such a judgement will be considerable.

In Canada, there has been an attempt to balance the powers of the Supreme Court and Parliament, and the idea of a dialogue between courts and legislature has been entertained.[2] Section 33 of the *Charter* gave Parliament or provincial legislatures the right to declare that an Act should operate notwithstanding provisions in the *Charter*. They can override the Court, although only for five years at a time. One controversial use of the override occurred in 1988 when Quebec refused to accept a ruling by the Supreme Court against a prohibition on languages other than French in shop signs. This was widely seen as a refusal by the Quebec Government to recognize basic rights, in this case that of native English speakers in the province. The outrage this produced illustrated the problems any government will face in challenging the Supreme Court in such matters. It seems that any judicial review of rights can give courts an almost unfettered discretion to decide how a society may operate. They are not constrained by the law, since they are in control of interpretations of it. They decide how far rights extend, and even what is a right. The issue is who is to decide on the kind of country citizens are to live in, supposedly impartial judges or elected representatives.

THE USE OF SUNDAY

Religion is one of the most sensitive areas courts can deal with. Judgements about the fair treatment of individuals, particularly when religious discrimination is alleged, will often collide with broader issues about the kind of society we want to live in. Questions about legal restrictions on what can be done on a Sunday have always been important for Christians. They may stop those of other religions, such as Jews, from working as they would wish. Yet the laws have also been designed for the public good, so that Sunday is not just preserved as a day of worship, but so that at least one day in the week could be a common day of rest. The traditional Christian Sabbath can be a secular day of rest.

Sunday legislation provided an early test for the Canadian *Charter*. In 1985 in *R. v. Big M Drug Mart,* the Canadian Supreme Court examined the purpose of the federal *Lord's Day Act*. The name alone suggests that the original Act had a religious purpose, and reflected the fact that Canada had regarded itself as a Christian country, laying down Christian standards in the conduct of public life. It was ironic that the *Charter*, designed particularly to protect the rights and freedoms of individuals, was invoked to allow a commercial company to operate on Sunday. The Court's basic finding was that the Act violated the *Charter* guarantee of freedom of conscience and religion. The basic objection was that 'religious values rooted in Christian morality are translated into a positive law binding on believers and non-believers alike'.[3] Favouring one religion was to be ruled out, and the Court struck down the Act in its entirety.

This finding made use of Article 2 of the *Charter*, stressing freedom of religion. The Court could not at that time rely on Section 15, guaranteeing equality under the law to all individuals, and 'in particular, without discrimination based on race, national or ethnic origin, colour, religion, sex, age, or mental or physical disability'. These were early days for the *Charter*, and Section 15 was not yet in force, in order to give time for public practices to be brought into line. One commentator says that this clause would more naturally have been used to strike down the Act. He says:

In my view, the objection to Sunday closing laws is really an equality claim . . . It is the favoured Christians who desire a Sunday Sabbath, over non-Christians who observe other Sabbaths, that provides the force of the constitutional argument.[4]

This means that appeals to ideas of equality, and the related, but vague, term of 'human dignity' are meant to justify the refusal by the law to favour one religion. Yet such 'Charter values' themselves need explanation. Equality is not a clear notion, although the idea of equality under the law has been a cherished notion of the common law. The idea that religions have to be treated equally, as opposed to their adherents being treated in a fair and non-discriminatory manner, is a more recent one. The argument is that it is not enough for everyone to be treated in the same way. It is an assault on the dignity of Jews to be expected to observe the Christian Sabbath. It would be possible to have Sunday closing laws, with exceptions, say, for Jewish traders, but an alternative is not to give preference to any one religion. That, however, must inevitably mean that religious considerations cannot influence public life, and that a Christian framework for society is steadily dismantled.

The Chief Justice of Canada calls equality 'the most difficult right' and favours what he terms 'substantive equality'.[5] He writes:

Substantive equality is founded on the principle that all human beings are of equal worth and possessed of the same innate human dignity, which the law must uphold and protect, not just in form but in substance . . . Substantive dignity is recognized worldwide as the governing legal paradigm.

The 1985 finding certainly followed the spirit of this, when it stated:

The Charter safeguards minorities from the threat of the 'tyranny of the majority'. To the extent that it binds all to a sectarian Christian idea, the *Lord's Day Act* works a form of coercion inimical to the spirit of the Charter and the dignity of all non-Christians.

This notion of dignity is often invoked, without any explanation of what justifies it. It is a fashionable concept, and like all fashions, could be discarded one day. It needs a substantial basis. Even if one can be given without resorting to religion, in traditionally Christian countries the idea has been inextricably linked with Christian teaching. The problem is how far it can be preserved once the religious context is removed. If it were based on a theistic, or even a Christian vision, using it to undermine the foundations on which it rests would be a dangerous enterprise.

The use of Sunday can never be a purely individual matter, since society as a whole has to come to a collective decision about public days of rest. Even in the United States, with its separation of Church and State, the Constitution specifically rules out Sundays as a day for official business. A minority may be prevented from behaving as they wish on a Sunday, but the alternative is for a majority to be forced to work on a day when they do not wish to. Indeed, according to the ideology of human rights, there should be something objectionable about Christians being forced to work on a Sunday whether they are in the majority or a minority.

The striking down of the entire *Lord's Day Act* suggested that the Supreme Court was more concerned about removing special privileges from Christianity than protecting rights. It was enough that the purpose of the act was to uphold Christian observance. In a subsequent case (*R. v. Edwards Books and Art Ltd*), the Supreme Court in Canada accepted that an Ontario Act restricting Sunday trading had an exclusively secular purpose, insisting on a secular day of rest, which just happened to be Sunday. It was therefore permissible. Yet reasons connected with the good of humanity can also be central to the religious reasons for a day of rest. The distinction between a religious Sabbath and a secular day of rest can be somewhat artificial.

Sunday Working

In recent years Sunday working and Sunday shopping have become more prevalent in Canada, the United Kingdom, and elsewhere. Market forces have proved powerful. Even if, however, the character of Sunday has changed, issues about the right of individuals to spend Sunday as they wish have not. One response to a pluralist society is to refuse to make any day special, but that does not solve the issue of people's right to manifest their religion. Unless everyone's rights are equally ignored, particular arrangements have to be made to suit their various needs. In a traditionally Christian country, ignoring the importance of Sunday to Christians erodes the possibility of it being used by communities as a day for worship.

What view should the law take when an employer demands work on Sunday as a condition of employment? Seven-day-week working has become more common for commercial reasons. The issue of what an employee is to do, who does not wish to work on a Sunday for religious reasons, surfaced in the England and Wales Court of Appeal in 2005. A long-term employee of a quarry firm was unwilling to change his work practices to include regular Sunday working. A new seven-day shift pattern was necessary to provide an increased level of production. He was eventually dismissed, although he had been offered alternative positions with lower pay. His claim to the employment tribunal was that 'I have been unfairly dismissed because I am a Christian'.

The Court of Appeal quoted precedents from the European Commission on Human Rights, whose functions have now been absorbed by the Strasbourg European Court. The position is summed up by Lord Justice Mummery, who reports concerning the European Convention on Human Rights:

There is a clear line of decisions by the Commission to the effect that Article 9 (on freedom of religion) is not engaged where an employee asserts Article 9 rights against his employer in relation to his hours working. The reason given is that if the employer's working practices and the employee's religious convictions are incompatible, the employee is free to resign in order to manifest his religious beliefs.

This, however, seems an extraordinary position to take about freedom of religion, which is an important right in the European Convention. As Lord Justice Mummery points out himself, issues about what school uniform an Islamic girl may be required to wear are not deemed by the Courts to be met by the reply that a girl can change schools. As Sunday working becomes more prevalent, those who wish to keep Sunday as a special day may find themselves progressively more restricted in the jobs they can undertake. In the case under discussion, conditions of employment demanding Sunday work were not known in advance, but were imposed after fourteen years' employment.

It may seem simple to say that employment contracts are freely entered into, and that those who do not like the terms should not take a job in the first place or resign. Many Christians will find that they have to choose between the best way of earning a living and their religious principles. The whole idea of basic rights is to protect people from this kind of choice. The retort that one can be free to manifest one's religion because one can freely choose to be unemployed is to dismiss the importance of any sincerely held religious beliefs. A right to freedom of religious practice may not be unqualified, but it is still a precious right. Much depends on how unreasonable it is to refuse particular terms of employment on the grounds of religious principle. In cases about Sunday working, European law holds that the commercial interests of an employer will always 'trump' the religious convictions of employees.

This type of case symbolizes disputes about the kind of society we live in. The protection of Sunday as a day of rest has long been an important element in English law, and such attitudes were transported to Canada. There was an assumption that English society, and its laws, rested on Christian assumptions, and that people were free to live their lives as they wished in a framework derived from those assumptions. The importance of freedom under the law was itself the result of a Christian emphasis. These principles go back into the mists of time, since before England was a unified kingdom, and certainly before it became associated with the other countries of the British Isles. Now, however, the view is suddenly gaining ground in some quarters that England is a secular society with no religious commitment underlying its institutions. This is legally and historically false. It is highly contentious even as a sociological observation, but the fact of the change is often just assumed.

Lord Justice Mummery notes in the Judgment on Sunday working that the position taken by the European Commission on Human Rights 'is that, so far as working hours are concerned, an employer is entitled to keep the work place secular'.[7] He considers that this must be regarded as the present state of the law, but, as he accepts, the House of Lords, or the Strasbourg Court, may have to revisit the issue. The Judge himself comments that 'in some sections of the community this is a controversial question which will not go away', and that 'its resolution requires a political solution'. Whatever new patterns of life emerge, it will surely be a continuing duty of the courts to protect individual liberty. Some work will always be essential on Sundays, but freedom of religion is meaningless if holding to Christian principles makes one unemployable.

CHARTER VALUES OR CHRISTIAN PRINCIPLES?

The path from a Christian to a secular country was mapped in the original judgement on Sunday trading by the Canadian Supreme Court. The judgement included the dictum that 'government may not coerce individuals to affirm a specific religious belief, or to manifest a specific religious practice for a sectarian purpose'.[8] Yet laws about Sunday did not force any-one to affirm any religious belief. Being given a day of rest is not the same as compulsory church attendance. Because the Court saw religious motivation in observing the 'Lord's Day', they immediately interpreted this as coercion. It certainly gave space for worship, but it also gave time for a myriad other activities as well. The Court might have reflected that true coercion lies in preventing people from attending worship because they have to work.

Law and Religion

The situation was summed up by the following part of the same judgement:

> In an earlier time, when people believed in the collective responsibility of the community toward some deity, the enforcement of religious conformity may have been a legitimate object of government, but since the *Charter*, it has become the right of every Canadian to work out for himself or herself what his or her religious obligations, if any, should be, and it is not for the state to dictate otherwise.[9]

The *Charter of Rights and Freedoms* brought about a sea change in Canadian society. Instead of religious beliefs being championed by society, the State has to be neutral between religions, and between belief and non-belief. The problem is whether the legally enforced absence of religion in the public square becomes itself tantamount to an official stance. It certainly implies the perceived public irrelevance of Christianity, and the act of withdrawing public recognition makes a clear statement. The same reasoning which saw Sunday observance as Christian tyranny also brought an end to religious instruction in State schools, and to public prayer in schools and city halls. Public acts, which assume Christian belief, are to be judged unconstitutional. Christians are prohibited from any religious practice in a public place. Because religion is regarded as a matter of private devotion, any conception of religion as having a social dimension, with an influence on communal and public life, has to be jettisoned.

The stress on individuals can be widened to include an acceptance of 'cultures'. As previously mentioned, Article 27 of the *Charter* refers to 'the multi-cultural heritage of Canadians'. This can become an added obstacle to passing any judgement on religious, or non-religious, beliefs. All must be accepted equally, to avoid discrimination, and the law degenerates into total relativism. We only have to ask whether this includes accepting the beliefs of those who do not value human equality to see the incoherence of the position. The State cannot be neutral about everything. 'Charter values' are being promulgated as a substitute for traditional Christian ones. They involve a substantive view of the world, which, right or wrong, is still very different from what Canada used to stand for.

The Preamble to the Canadian *Charter* suggests something quite different. Its opening phrase reads: 'Whereas Canada is founded upon principles that recognise the supremacy of God and the rule of law . . .', and then there follows the guarantee of rights and freedoms. The rule of law is associated with God's supremacy and there appears to be a suggestion that justice is linked to religious belief, and that public law is ultimately validated by divine authority. Yet the Preamble has been deliberately ignored by the courts, and even pronounced a 'dead-letter' by the British Columbian Court of Appeal in 1999. As one writer has put it: 'Far from being a dead-letter, the Preamble poses fundamental questions of political philosophy, including the relationship between the transcendental and political order.'[10] It indicates that far from religion being a threat to 'Charter values', the whole idea of a just society, underpinned by the rule of law, has religious roots, which perhaps themselves need nurturing. The Canadian Courts have taken it upon themselves to ignore any such philosophical grounding, in the interests of a new form of 'multiculturalism'.

No clause in Canada's constitution forbids a religious establishment, and there is no constitutional ground for keeping religion and the State wholly separate. The Courts have chosen to interpret the Preamble in terms of their understanding of the necessities of a multicultural Canada, rather than looking at the law in the context of the Preamble. The Supreme Court alleged in the Sunday trading case that the Preamble made no explicit reference to the Christian God.[11] Yet in the light of Canada's religious history, it is hard to see what other God is being invoked. As one writer comments:

Incorporated in the final draft at the last minute as a result of Evangelical lobbying, as a compromise to secure Western Canadian support, many Christians in Canada think that the Preamble means that the laws should reflect Christian moral values.[12]

Nothing could be further from the truth from the point of view of the Courts.

It is one thing to ignore the Preamble, or to say that it does not cohere with substantive provisions. It is another to pretend that it does not refer to the Christian God. The latter is referred to on Canadian coins by the initials 'D.G.' (Dei Gratia), referring to Elizabeth II, 'by the grace of God', Queen. The same initials occur on the coins of the United Kingdom where they accompany the Latin initials 'F.D.' ('Fidei Defensor'—'Defender of the Faith'). The Christian faith is there explicitly invoked, and there can be little doubt that Canada, at least at that symbolic level, still acknowledges the Christian God. No doubt for Charter reasons, some would want to remove the reference to God even from the coins, but that would merely illustrate the fundamental challenge to Canada's religious and constitutional heritage being surreptitiously made. Issues which used to be the province of a democratically elected Parliament are given over to judges. Once it was made clear by the Canadian Supreme Court that no religion or belief system could have a privileged position, Christianity's historic position, and its role in public life, had to be changed.

TEACHING TRADITIONAL MORALITY

In 1994 the Ontario Court of Appeal rejected an argument by parents from different faiths that their religious freedom was infringed because the secular curriculum of public schools was opposed to religious values. They wanted alternative religious schools financed by public school boards. The Court's reply was: 'The public school system is now secular. Its goal is to educate, not indoctrinate...Secularism is not coercive; it is neutral.'[13] That was the end of a process in which a vaguely Protestant school system was transformed, with religious observance outlawed. Because of a quirk of history, provision of Roman Catholic schools in Ontario is still guaranteed by the Constitution, an inequality in provision which is resented in some quarters, and was criticized in 1999 by the United Nations Human Rights Committee.

The view expressed about the neutrality of secularism is naïve. The state claims to be neutral because it regards religion as a private matter. Yet the freedom which this allows does not extend to allowing parental choice in State schools in the matter of religious education. The State, it seems, knows best, and following judicial interpretations of the *Charter*, it also appears that the State has no need of any theological support. Yet the idea that all religions are of equal importance and have no place in the public sphere is itself a very distinctive position. A distinct ideology is purveyed, with the result that many parents turn away to a private education, which can be religiously based.

The rights and freedoms guaranteed by the Canadian *Charter* can conflict with each other. The demand for equality may collide with the requirement for freedom of conscience and religion. Even though there are Catholic schools, they are not immune from the reach of the *Charter*. In 2002, a Catholic school in Ontario was taken before the courts when the principal tried to stop a male student taking his boyfriend to his high school prom, on the grounds that he could not endorse conduct contrary to Catholic teaching. A court injunction was granted at the last moment preventing the principal from acting in this way. One legal writer comments with approval:

The idea that matters affecting women, gays and lesbians, transgendered persons, and so on, even child sexuality, could be equality issues rather than morality issues, is evidence of the sea change in legal perception made in large part by the Charter, and the way courts have adjudicated cases decided under it.[14]

In other words, equality is not seen as a matter of morality, but somehow distinct from it. Perhaps it is seen as a public, procedural, issue, in contrast to morality being a matter of private choice. To an onlooker, however, it looks as if a powerful new morality is being preached, so powerful that it will justify restricting people's religious liberty if they try to transgress it. It dictates standards of behaviour to a religious school which was acting in accordance with its traditional teaching. The *Charter* itself did not explicitly refer to sexual orientation, but the Supreme Court accepted in 1995 that it was a ground of discrimination analogous to those which are mentioned in Article 15, dealing with equality. This may even make it difficult for Churches and other bodies to teach that homosexual behaviour is morally wrong. 'Charter values' are on a collision course with the traditional religious understanding not just of the Roman Catholic Church, but of other branches of Christianity, and other religions, such as Islam. The same writer comments:

The very teaching of homophobic doctrine is a homophobic act, and in any public context should be impermissible. It ought not to be the practice of any state actor, religious or otherwise. It should be permitted, if at all, only in a specifically religious context.[15]

Thus the demand for equal treatment of citizens has quickly become extended to a threat to the moral teaching of much traditional religion. In so far as a Canadian school receives money from the State, it has to conform to the legal principles of the *Charter*, as interpreted by judges. Religion is forced to retreat first from public life, and then from the control of its own institutions according to its own standards. The idea that everyone has a right to equal respect quickly degenerates into a prohibition on criticizing other people's views or behaviour on moral grounds. That can be seen as a refusal to grant them proper dignity. If someone takes offence, the right to express religious views can be quickly removed. 'Equality' becomes favoured over religious liberty. 'Neutrality' becomes a restraint on religion. The removal of religiously based reasoning from public affairs quickly reaches into private spaces.

SAME-SEX MARRIAGE

Some of these arguments might seem specific to Canada, but similar issues arise in many jurisdictions. Traditions can be quickly swept aside by the application of ideas of individual equality, and a prohibition of discrimination. One of the most fraught examples of this comes in arguments about whether a State should allow marriage between persons of the same sex. Marriage concerns the most private of relationships, and yet is itself a public and legally recognized act. It is not surprising that conflicts over the relationship between private and public should be at their most obvious here. Until recently, it was taken for granted that marriage was between people of opposite sex, and dictionary definitions reflected that. With growing public acceptance of homosexuality, the idea of marriage between persons of the same sex has been gaining currency. The United Kingdom has tried to side-step a direct assault on the religious understanding of the nature of marriage by introducing in 2005 the status of 'civil partnership'.

The stage is set in several countries for a major collision between law and religion. Once again, Canada has been one of the trail-blazers, and the Canadian Government referred the matter of same-sex marriage to the Supreme Court in advance of legislation. In such situations, it can ask for advisory opinions about the interpretation of the Constitution. Two particular questions were addressed to the Court in 2003, and answered in 2004. Firstly, they asked whether extending the capacity to marry to persons of the same sex was consistent with the Canadian *Charter of Rights and Freedoms*. Secondly, the Court was asked whether the *Charter*'s guarantee of freedom of religion would protect religious officials from being compelled to perform a marriage between two persons of the same sex, contrary to their religious beliefs.

The very fact that the second question could be asked is an indication of how law and religion can collide. Marriage is a public act, ratified by the State, but at the same time it can be seen as a religious one (even a 'sacrament' for some Christians).

As with problems over divorce, a legal view about marriage can conflict with a religious one. Can clergy be compelled to conduct same-sex marriages? The Canadian Supreme Court ruled that it would be a violation of freedom of religion, as guaranteed by section (2a) of the *Charter* to force them to act against their principles.[16] It also accepted that the compulsory use of 'sacred places' would be a violation of the *Charter*. Yet the substantive issue remained. The proposed Act of Parliament wanted to define marriage for civil persons as 'the lawful union of two persons to the exclusion of all others'. In other words is their sex irrelevant?

The Court quotes a statement from a case of 1866 (*Hyde v. Hyde*) which held that 'marriage, as understood in Christendom, may for this purpose be defined as the voluntary union for life of one man and one woman, to the exclusion of all others'.[17] This is in essence the common law tradition, but the Court's commentary goes to the heart of modern problems about the relation of religion and society. It picks up the reference to 'Christendom' and remarks that *Hyde* 'spoke to a society of shared social values where marriage and religion were thought to be inseparable'.[18] It flatly denies that such a situation still holds, calling Canada 'a pluralistic society'. It goes on to say: 'Our Constitution is a living tree, which by way of progressive interpretation, accommodates and addresses the realities of modern life.' Thus, they continue, 'Our Constitution succeeds in its ambitious enterprise, that of structuring the exercise of power by the organs of state in times vastly different from those in which it was crafted.'[19] This is the edge of a vast controversy in jurisprudence about how far constitutional interpretation must reflect the times in which it takes place. Can a Constitution really change with the times?

In the Canadian case, it was for Parliament to pass an Act about marriage. Nevertheless, the decision that the meaning of 'marriage' was not fixed forever helped to create a new situation in which it could do that. The Supreme Court was faced with the objection that same-sex marriage was unnatural, and stretched the Constitution beyond 'natural limits'. Its answer was that the argument could only succeed if some 'objective core' of meaning could be identified which defines what is 'natural' in relation to marriage.[20] The Court held that the only 'objective core' which those before the Court agreed was that marriage was 'the voluntary union of two people to the exclusion of all others'. Views otherwise diverge, and the Court was faced with competing opinions on the natural limits of marriage. This argument implies that we simply have to concentrate on what everyone can agree is acceptable. On this model, all that is required for arguments about polygamy to succeed is that groups of people make representations to the Court showing that they do not agree with current prejudices in favour of monogamy. The same argument can be used for the legitimation of under-age marriages, or even legal unions with animals. There are ultimately no limits on what, for the Court, can count as marriage. In the present case, too, even on the Court's own assumptions, it looks as if they were optimistic about any core of agreement. To say that a disagreement between those who champion same-sex marriage and those who rule it out has a common core of agreement about a voluntary union between persons, is merely to decide the case in favour of same-sex marriage. So far from settling on a common denominator between the two sides, the Court has had to make a simple choice between two positions.

The extension of the right to marry to couples of the same sex is seen as an application of the ideal of individual equality, but this goes to the heart of issues of what is meant by a society. A wider understanding of marriage could be socially beneficial, but that is never argued. No religion can be indifferent to what constitutes proper human flourishing, and, in particular, to the issue of what provision is made for the care and education of children.[21] The common law tradition was sensitive to that, but if it is to be overturned because of its Christian roots, we have entered new territory. Arguments in Canada foreshadow disputes in the United States. In Canada the law has come to depend on the prevailing consensus, and in so far as it is controlled by judges, the consensus need only be that of an intellectual elite. That, however, is a fickle, and unreliable, basis for the organization of society.

9

Religion in State Education

SHOULD RELIGION BE TAUGHT?

THE ISSUE of whether religion is a public or private matter becomes particularly controversial when its place in schools is considered. Parents often want their children's education to take place in an explicitly religious context. Many countries, however, are reluctant to give any official sanction to religious teaching. They view the support of, or encouragement of, any religious activities as alien to their function. This has, in different countries, encouraged the spread of private, religious, schools where parents can educate their children in their chosen faith. Many fear the disintegration of society, when this begins to happen, because they do not want separate communities solidified in what should be one society. However, it is regarded as a basic human right, spelt out in Article 26 of the Universal Declaration of Human Rights, that 'parents have a prior right to choose the kind of education that shall be given to their children'. Even so, there is often a reluctance to fund religious schools for different faiths, but instead to encourage all to attend a common school.

Parents have lost confidence in schools' ability to deal with religious matters, not just in countries such as Canada, with its secularism, but even in England where religious education is still regarded as having an official place in State schools. One underlying cause has been the influence of philosophical views suggesting that religion was not susceptible to public verification, and therefore could not be concerned with truth. Because religious 'truth' was not viewed like scientific truth and did not seem to deal with 'facts', the temptation has been to consign religion to the individual sphere. These doubts tended to crystallize in the 1960s, when, both theology and educational theory felt the need to try and provide answers about the place of religion in the face of the apparently remorseless advance of scientific standards for knowledge. It was an age when radical theology reached a wide audience in Britain through the publication of such popular books as *Honest to God* by the then Bishop of Woolwich. In education, to take one example, a prominent academic in the field, Paul Hirst, posed the following question in 1965:

The fundamental philosophical question that arises for religious education in maintained schools is surely whether or not there is in religion a form of publicly accepted knowledge or belief that is appropriate for these schools to hand on.[1]

Maintained schools were publicly funded schools, and the question arose from philosophical doubts that religion could be publicly established in the way that physics could be. Yet the very idea of 'publicly accepted knowledge' slides from a philosophical issue of knowledge depending on public verification to the sociological point that there was more disagreement about religion in society. This later became mingled with a concern about the position of immigrants to Britain from non-Christian societies. All this tended to weaken traditional assumptions in Britain about the place of Christianity in schools.

The previous writer was himself in no doubt how to answer the question he had posed. He said: 'If in fact, as seems to be the case at present, there are no agreed public tests whereby true and false can be distinguished in religious claims, then we can hardly maintain that we have a domain of knowledge and truth.'[2] This assertion itself seems to be ambiguous as between a philosophical claim and a sociological observation. Yet such positions were not peculiar to the 1960s but have even become orthodoxy in the field of religious education. A contemporary writer, Robert Jackson, advocates approaches which 'avoid the propagation of any religious or secular view'.[3] This is because, he says, 'they acknowledge that the truth of religious claims is not publicly demonstrable, and that the answer to the question of ultimate truth cannot be, at present at least, resolved'. This last phrase implies a social and political situation which could change, but he had previously referred to 'particular epistemologies and values'. That suggests that the difficulty is more deep-rooted.

Just because we may not all agree about something does not mean that there is nothing to agree about, or that some ways of approaching the issue are not better than others. Reality must always constrain us. Yet educationalists are very prone to jump from the lack of agreement about religion to a child-centred approach which stresses the autonomy of the pupil. We are therefore told of the importance of maintaining 'an epistemological openness, encouraging children and young people to express and formulate their own positions'.[4]

One danger, which some warn against, is of seeing religions and cultures as entities with distinct boundaries, so that there are insiders and outsiders. That kind of position can encourage a relativism which sees particular 'truths' as the preserves of each entity. There would be truths for Christians, other truths for Muslims, and so on. When religions co-exist in the same society, the idea of self-contained entities becomes implausible when one can see different influences at work on the same individual. This can be used as an argument for reinforcing a stress on the autonomy of the individual. The school then becomes a place where a personal search for meaning is encouraged without the standards of any particular world-view being imposed. The aim, we are told, is rather to help young people find their own position.

In one sense, all good education involves students being given the skills to make their own judgements in a particular subject. The ability to examine received position in a rational and critical manner is crucial. This educational point coalesces with the religious belief in the importance of freedom. Genuine religious belief must be chosen, not imposed. Yet in science, not to mention other disciplines such as history, the importance of personal judgement cannot be allowed to eclipse the fact that no individual can simply manufacture evidence. There is, for example, a difference between history and writing a novel. Is religion any different? Children may well be encouraged to think for themselves in relation to it, but education cannot be satisfied with that, without lapsing into an extreme subjectivism. Criticism has to be informed. Critical thinking cannot take place in a vacuum, but must be about something. In the case of religion, there would have to be knowledge of at least one tradition.

INDOCTRINATION OR SELF-DEVELOPMENT?

The view that 'religions' have no sharp boundaries can be made an excuse for concentrating on children's reactions to the world, and their own attempts to find meaning, rather than properly introducing them to the rich traditions of a particular religion, except at the most superficial level. The result is that current religious education in Britain often in practice does little to inform children about the nature of Christianity, or give them even the most basic facts about its teaching. The word 'spirituality' is invoked in this connection. When understood in a traditional way, it can evoke ideas of reacting to transcendent reality, and to God in particular. When understood in a subjectivist fashion, however, it can mean nothing more than an aesthetic experience or 'wonder'. Religious education then becomes not much more than a laudable attempt to stretch children's imaginations beyond the demands of a narrow examination-led curriculum.

Behind many of the debates about teaching religion in the second half of the twentieth century lay the fear of 'indoctrination'. As Jackson summarizes the development of religious education in that period, there has been a move from what he terms 'types of non-denominational Christian nurture' in ordinary State schools in England and Wales.[5] Instead, he says, there is what he describes as 'a non-indoctrinatory study of the main religions represented in Britain with the goal of developing understanding, linked to reflection by pupils on their studies, geared up to the promotion of personal development'. 'Indoctrination' normally carries with it the implication of coercion, and the abuse of power. Perhaps teaching a religion 'as true' may seem to be in that category. Someone cannot be forced to have a faith, but they can be informed what the faith is faith in. The message can all too easily be given that religion is a matter of arbitrary personal commitment, and that truth is not at stake. Religion is then converted from being a matter of major public concern, to something that is concerned only with 'personal development'. Reason has no role to play, since there are no better or worse ways of developing, just different ones.

The accusation of indoctrination did not spring from any perceived compulsion. It came from the fact that religious views which were seen as controversial, and not publicly justifiable, were presented as having a claim to truth. They were being treated on a par with scientific subjects, where teaching the laws of physics would not be regarded as indoctrination. The idea, too, that pupils must make their own decisions about religion may seem admirable, but the autonomy encouraged was of an extreme kind. They were not being left free to decide whether to accept or reject the alleged truths of Christianity. Traditional education should have done that. Instead, children and young people were encouraged to decide what should be true for them. Once one gets into the realm of what is often vaguely called 'beliefs and values', one should, it appears, not merely make up one's mind. One should have control over what there is to make up one's mind about.

Religious education can become an exercise in narcissistic subjectivity, with an emphasis on a person's search for meaning, rather than on the nature of the reality we all confront. These are trends which can show themselves to a greater or lesser extent. Some practitioners in religious, or 'spiritual' education are explicitly relativist. Two writers on education are not afraid of that label, saying that we construct the world.[6] We do not discover it. They sum up their position when they claim: 'For faith to be faith it can have no object. The same is true of values.'[7] The point is that they only have subjects, and are about the people who possess them. The world is a reflection of belief. This is an extreme position in theories about religious education, but it is the logical conclusion of a tendency that has grown. Many educationalists have felt that the only way to preserve a child's autonomy is not to make truth claims, or even admit that religions aspire to truth.

Too many educationalists have too easily assumed that faith is either taught or it is not. Indeed, precisely because they discounted claims to truth, they have failed to take seriously the way in which religion can be rationally examined and discussed. Even though there is a clear distinction between learning about a religion, and being forced to adopt it, there is a deep-set fear that educating children about Christianity, and, say, the contents of the Bible, is somehow an attempt to make them Christian. The increasing presence of other religions, such as Islam, in England, also gives strength to the familiar argument that no one religion should be favoured, but all must be treated equally.

Even countries such as France and the United States recognize that education has a vital role in promoting understanding between religions, at a time of increasing religious conflict across the world. The neutrality of their schools on religious matters should not mean that religion is an unmentionable subject, although it often does. The French Presidential Commission on '*laïcité*', which we have already discussed, remarks that 'a better mutual understanding of different culture and traditions of religious thought is today essential'.[8] They look to a better integration of teaching on religious matters with other subjects such as history. In the same spirit, a 1998 Circular from the U.S. Department of Education says that 'public schools may not provide religious instruction, but they may teach about religion, including the Bible or other scripture'. This distinction between instruction and 'teaching about' goes to the heart of the matter from an American point of view.

Guidelines circulated to American teachers say: 'Though schools must be neutral with respect to religion, they may play an active role with respect to teaching civic values and virtue, and the moral code that holds us together as a community.'[9] This, however, creates a problem. Many of the same objections to religious teaching can be levied in any pluralist society against the deliberate teaching of a particular morality. Both could be said to depend on controversial beliefs which cannot command universal agreement. Both involve a challenge to the autonomy of the child in creating a personal belief-system. Moreover, many believe that morality cannot be so easily prised apart from religious understandings. It is difficult to talk of morality in the abstract, in isolation from a more general world-view, religious or not, about human nature, and our place in the world.[10] Kent Greenawalt, writing on American education is in no doubt that just as schools teach physical facts, they should teach 'that members of different races, and women and men, are fundamentally equal'.[11] Yet it seems that they cannot discuss reasons why this is so, as they could be religious. Greenawalt is keen to promote the view, underpinned by much current American law, that 'religion should be treated fairly, but the state should have no position about religious propositions'.[12] For fear of any particular belief being promoted, he says that he doubts 'that a critical discussion in school of the strengths and weaknesses of various religious perspectives is generally a good idea'.[13] Even teaching about the Bible is dangerous, (despite its cultural and literary import- ance), because, he says: 'A Bible course reinforces the notion that Christianity is by far the most important religion.'[14]

Any State may be tempted to leave religion alone in this way, but a pluralist society particularly has to encourage toler- ance and respect for diversity. Some educationalists refer to 'procedural values', the values of toleration and mutual respect, on which democracy depends.[15] Jackson refers to them as 'non- negotiable', saying that they are the fundamental rights and duties that recognize the equal worth and dignity of all, upon which liberal democracy is based. Liberalism advocates a free society, but it cannot let education be so free that the preser- vation of freedom is left to chance. It wants to hold that all 'values' are personal, but sees that some are 'non-negotiable' and have to be positively taught. Underlying all this is the large issue of the basis of ideas of equality and dignity. If it is even possible that they have to be based on religious beliefs, the liberal has a problem. They could then only be taught in a religious context or not taught at all.

CELEBRATING DIVERSITY

Arguments about how far religion is a fit subject for public education become more acute in a country such as England, because religious education remains by law part of the curricu- lum. The 1988 Education Reform Act stated that the syllabuses for religious education must 'reflect the fact that the religious traditions in Great Britain are in the main Christian, whilst taking account of the other principal religions represented in Great Britain'.[16] Yet current religious education tends to be 'multi-faith', and it is commonplace for British pupils to leave school with little understanding of Christianity, let alone the specific teaching of Christ in the New Testament. Even given the view that one should only 'teach about' religion, this is unsatisfactory. Much great art and music has centred around Christian themes, and children who are ignorant of them are culturally illiterate, unable to understand the significance of a painting by Rubens of the Nativity, or of Bach's St. Matthew Passion.

Despite the emphasis in the 1988 Act on Christianity, the words of which have been echoed subsequently, a non-statutory framework for religious education, published in 2004, gives little prominence to it as a religion, and none to knowledge of the Bible, the literature of which has had at least as profound an effect on the English language as the works of Shakespeare. The foreword by the relevant government minister, the Secretary of State for Education and Skills, says firmly that the focus of the framework 'is to set out a system that places value on the ethos and morals that religious educa-tion can establish, independent of any faith'.[17] Christianity, it seems, can be easily put aside in pursuit of more important goals in religious education. The latter's role is not to inform pupils about a religion whose influence is still pervasive in the society in which they are growing up. Morality can, it seems, be taught apart from any particular religion, and, the document begins, religious education 'actively promotes the values of truth, justice, respect for all and care of the environment'. Particular emphasis is placed on 'pupils valuing themselves and others; the role of the family; the celebration of diversity in society through understanding similarities and differences' and also 'the sustainable development of the earth'. All this may be admirable, but it clearly comprises a specific agenda.

'The celebration of diversity' may be a laudable political aim in a society where a government may be afraid of smouldering racial and religious tensions. Matters are not helped, however, by the surreptitious extension of the idea of religion to include 'religions and beliefs'.[18] This picks up phrases we have previously seen used in connection with human rights, but it blurs the focus of 'religious education' very considerably. It also raises a question of what limits there might be to diversity. Is all difference to be celebrated, no matter what the content of the beliefs? Since pupils must be ready 'to value difference and diversity for the common good', there is a presumption that we can all recognize what constitutes the 'common' good without reference to religion. Yet some systems of belief may have no conception of such a thing, but may be exclusively concerned with their own purposes. Are they to be celebrated? The document points out that 'respect for all' involves 'appreciating that some beliefs are not inclusive and considering the issues this raises for individuals and society'.[19] Given that the document wants to stress 'the significance of interfaith dialogue', the implication is that non-inclusive beliefs are probably going to be a threat to the 'common good' and 'community cohesion'.[20]

What is meant, however, by saying that beliefs are not inclusive? Exclusive beliefs are normally seen as those which assert truth in such a way that those who do not share them must be regarded as mistaken. Claims to truth are liable to involve claims to priority of one religion over others. They are going to be divisive, because they imply some views are right and others wrong, and that one religion might be preferable to another. The following pronouncement would therefore be regarded as presumptuous:

When a society is in flux ... there is a renewed hunger for that which endures and gives meaning. The Christian church can speak uniquely to that need, for at the heart of our faith stands the conviction that all people, irrespective of race, background and circumstances, can find lasting significance and purpose in the Gospel of Jesus Christ.[21]

This involves a claim to universal truth, which must cut across any celebration of diversity for its own sake. Yet this was not an idle, irresponsible claim. It is what Christians have traditionally believed, and it was made by Queen Elizabeth II in her capacity not only as Head of State, but Supreme Governor of the Church of England, whose General Synod she was addressing. As we have seen, Islam makes similar exclusive claims to truth. Yet any approach that regards such claims to truth as 'an issue', or a problem concerning the common good (itself a phrase with a Christian pedigree) must impose an alien ideology on much religion. Religious education no longer accepts religion on its own terms, but in effect becomes an ideological tool, as a government faces problems about social divisions.

Four attitudes are listed in the National Framework for Religious Education as 'essential for good learning in religious education'.[22] They are 'self awareness', a very subjectivist idea, 'respect for all', to value diversity, 'open-mindedness', a philosophical rather than a religious virtue, and 'appreciation and wonder'. The latter could pave the way to religion, but there is little to indicate precisely what should be appreciated, or the direction wonder should lead us. All these may be good qualities, but they are about the pupil and not reality. The reiterated value of diversity, and the importance of positively appreciating differences in others, all contribute to a position which is itself far from neutral. It is seeking to teach, or indoctrinate, a set of views regarded as necessary in a liberal and pluralist democracy. As such, it will satisfy few. Some who are suspicious of religion in the classroom may prefer philosophy in schools, to help pupils be open-minded, and to think clearly about wider issues about meaning and purpose. On the other hand, religious believers of different faiths will find their children being given a set of attitudes which imply that any religion, or belief, is as good as any other. No way, in particular, is laid down for communicating the tenets of the Christian faith to children who have to grow up in a country which, according to the 2002 census, was still 72% Christian. They need to have some understanding of the traditions and cultural assumptions which surround them, and which are still imbued with Christian attitudes.

THE ROLE OF TRADITION

These issues may seem specific to the British context, but the basic problem is pervasive in pluralist democracies. There is the constant temptation to regard all claims to truth as socially divisive, and a desire, in the name of 'inclusion', to accept all 'religions and beliefs'. There must always be a tension between respecting and celebrating diversity, and taking any religion's claims to truth seriously. Yet all religions cannot be right, and some of them may even advocate what has to be unacceptable in a civilized society. Furthermore, once the encouragement of toleration slides into an acceptance of anything, all religion will gradually appear worthless. Why believe anything, if all beliefs are equally valid? That only has the result of implying that none are. Critics, indeed, of the kind of religious education which is 'multi-faith' allege that it is not the result of growing secularism, but is itself a contributory factor in its formation.

A paradox about some forms of relativism is that, although they deny objective truth, they do stress the role of collective standards in a society. The issue is then what counts as the relevant society in the particular context. Certainly any challenge to the idea of a truth holding for everyone leaves vague the issue of how one relativizes truth. It might be possible to suppose that the dominant tradition of a society sets the standards, and should be transmitted through the teaching in State schools. A religion is then taught not on the grounds that it is true, but because it is the religion of that society. Christianity could then be upheld simply because it was inseparable from an idea of England. Traditionalists in many societies take a similar line, but it can be a source of dogmatism and intolerance. Yet this perhaps illustrates the danger of discarding ideas of truth and rationality. The alternative may be the imposition of some conformity through the exercise of power. No objective standards would be left to judge this morally wrong. Relativists can only pass on the tradition that has given them identity. There is no way it could be assessed in a cool or rational manner, since there is nowhere for them to stand apart from the standards and presuppositions they already possess. Relativism and reason can have nothing to do with each other.

If religion is divorced from its ability to claim truth, its most important characteristic has been ignored. The fear of 'indoctrination' can quickly degenerate in a reluctance to engage with religious claims on their own terms. This does not result in an openness to all religion, so much as ignorance and indifference. Rationality cannot be equated with a detachment from religion. Only by wrestling with questions of truth can anyone see the reasons for and against holding certain beliefs. Claims to truth invite criticism and rational assessment. Imposing conformity of belief is wrong, but so is contempt for the possibility of truth. Relativism has this much right on its side, in that the traditions which have helped form us and our surroundings do matter. Even if we eventually wish to reject them, we need to understand them. Neutrality quickly becomes the kind of indifference which results in an unthinking betrayal of tradition. Yet on the other hand an unquestioning acceptance of tradition will also fail to take truth seriously.

Education has to walk a tightrope. At one extreme, it could involve the unquestioning imposition of a set of beliefs through the exercise of arbitrary power. That must involve the removal of personal freedom. It is a mistake to imagine that the only alternative is such absolute individual freedom that no-one has to learn anything, not even what a religion claims to be about. Rationality may presuppose freedom, but it also entails that we have material to reason about. A relativist stress on the importance of tradition in forming attitudes may go too far in accepting the presuppositions of a society unconditionally. All tradition has to be judged by reason, and reason has not itself been simply formed by tradition. We can surely learn to detach ourselves from our context in order to assess it. Good education should always have the aim of developing that critical faculty. Such rational criticism need not be negative since it can also serve to see the importance of tradition.

The truth hidden in a post-modernist stress on the way we are formed by our historical context is that no-one ever reasons in a vacuum. Reason has to start somewhere. To adopt an adage of pragmatist philosophy, we have to start from where we are. We do not have, though, to finish there. Our own traditions, and the beliefs and pre-suppositions of a society, have to be our starting-point. In England, a neutral education system, treating all traditions as of equal relevance, cuts children off from the ingrained assumptions of their own society. An educational system which stresses diversity, rather than the undoubted fact of an ongoing Christian tradition, fails to pass on a central aspect of English culture. Even those from other backgrounds need to understand the significance of the Christian background of the country in which they live. This is a matter of informing, not indoctrinating.

AUSTRALIAN INDIVIDUALISM

Concern about whether, and how, to teach about religion in schools is world-wide. An educationalist in Australia shows the same presuppositions as others when he faces the problem about how to teach in a pluralist society. The aim of religious education is, he considers, 'to offer students resources for their individual spiritual quest, rather than dogmatic answers'.[23] Conclusions about the truth or falsity of any belief system would be premature, and the point of teaching is for students to be 'brought to a point of personal commitment to beliefs and values that they have chosen for themselves on good grounds'.[24] It is not clear where the standards for such 'good grounds' are to come from. Certainly the emphasis is on empowering individuals, to avoid the dreaded 'indoctrination'.

Religion in State Education

The author is fearful of any form of coercion, and is extremely critical of any common worship, even in specifically religious schools. He sees it as a 'grievous infringement of individual liberty', holding that this kind of compulsion can only 'poison the spirit.'[25] Furthermore, he complains, 'if it succeeds in conditioning the student to an uncritical group loyalty, it is an evil spirit'. The idea of common worship, and prayers in schools, has been controversial for many years in several countries, and individuals should, and normally do, have the right not to participate. It is therefore not so much the compulsory nature of the worship, as the fact that it takes place at all in an educational setting, which is provoking criticism. It is, however, far from clear that young people who have no experience of Christian worship, will have any clear idea of what they are rejecting. In a country with a Christian heritage, that may be a cause for concern. The provision of such worship can be seen as part of an educational process, which extends, rather than limits, freedom of choice. That, however, assumes that such worship can be valuable. Atheists may not think it is, but in that case it becomes obvious that the argument is one about the possible truth of Christianity, not individual freedom.

The writer considers that nothing can be presented as true in the field of religion, for fear of introducing any coercion into the process. Yet although the abuse of authority is one thing, the problem is that truth is the greatest authority of all, and the writer is very near ignoring its relevance because it is a threat to freedom. The perceived danger of 'preaching' in schools can soon become a refusal to acknowledge even that a religion sees itself as claiming truth. The price of liberty can soon appear to be nihilism, and that is an incoherent position. If nothing matters, freedom certainly does not.

Despite a personal distaste for relativism, he contents himself with observing that 'it is a position which can be disputed'.[26] As such it should not be assumed in any teaching, but neither should its contrary. Thus not only must students be free to decide their own religious stance, but they can also be free to decide whether there is such a thing as truth. He writes that the student should be 'free to exercise a reasoned choice as to whether to take a relativist or an absolutist position vis-a-vis religious belief and commitment'.[27] This begs the question whether reasoned choices are conceivable without the idea of truth. What would make a choice better or worse from a rational standpoint, if it was made in a total vacuum, unconstrained by any demands from the real world? If the relativism envisaged is limited to religion, that depends on the controversial view that, unlike other assertions, religious language cannot claim truth.[28]

The concern for freedom in the face of possible coercion leads to an unbridled individualism, whereby any collective activity, such as worship, looks a threat. No society, however, can function without some level of agreement, and it needs shared rituals and common loyalties. Schools have traditionally helped to mould those, and even today stress on classes in 'citizenship' is an admission that personal liberty is not enough. Respect for it has to be nurtured in a common framework.

Our Australian author believes that to be 'fair and effective', religious education, whether in government or private schools, 'must be compatible with good democratic theory'.[29] This is to imply that democracy involves an aggressive individualism, extolling a radical freedom according to which we each decide not just what to believe, but what actually shall be true (for us).

Yet democratic theory cannot mould our ideas of truth. The latter under-gird our democracy in the first place. It is because we believe in individual freedom that democracy follows. We depend on prior metaphysical and religious beliefs about human nature. If freedom and rights, even children's rights, become the only measure of an educational system, it begins to operate in a dangerous vacuum. Little remains to keep a society together.

Freedom can be challenged, and rights can be ignored. When that happens, what resources has any educational system transmitted to see why this is wrong and to be resisted? Any idea that they belong to a wider community, which may help to give them their identity, or that tradition may be valuable, has been passed over. Everyone's judgement has become as good as any other's. Assuming that religion is irrelevant to any good democratic education, and may even be an obstacle to it, again raises the basic issue of why democracy matters. Yet as we have seen, the demand for individual autonomy is rooted as much in religious ideas about free will as anything. Using democratic theory as a way of restricting the influence of Christianity may in the end prove self-destructive. Some of the strongest roots of democracy could thereby be destroyed.

10

Must We Privatize Religion?

THE PRESTIGE OF SCIENCE

NOT LONG ago it was assumed that the ebbing of faith, when confronted by the insights of modern science, would soon deprive religion of all its influence; 'secularization' was assumed to be an inevitable trend. Those living in many Western European countries may find that still confirmed in their everyday experience, but Western Europe can be very untypical of the rest of the world. The impact of a militant Islam is felt in many places, and at the same time Christian belief is spreading in Africa and Asia in ways that would be astonishing to European Christians resigned to seemingly inexorable decline. In the United States, organized Christianity is strong, but interestingly encounters the same kind of philosophical opposition which seems so much more effective in Europe. There are constant pressures there for the complete privatization of religion.

When we examine the main currents in contemporary thought challenging the public recognition of religion, an obvious one is a respect for science and scientists as the sole source of established knowledge. While across the world, and within most countries, there is a wide range of religious and anti-religious beliefs, science appears as a settled body of knowledge, with recognized procedures for resolving differences. In contrast, religion appears to collapse into a cacophony of diverse attitudes and practices, often intolerant of each other.

The divergence between the two spheres can seem so striking that from the time of the later Enlightenment in the eighteenth century, there has been a strong tendency to see the realm of science as exclusively the realm of reason. 'Faith' can be made to appear something totally different, to be seen indeed as a menace to the establishment of a shared rationality. The narrowing of the English word 'science' to mean only empirical investigation with its agreed procedures would seem to be part of the process. The Latin 'scientia', referring to knowledge in general, has become restricted to what was once seen only as a part of knowledge. The implication, sometimes made explicit, is that 'faith', particularly of a religious kind, cannot embody any knowledge. Perhaps it tells us more about the attitudes of those who espouse it, than about the reality confronting us all.

Some see science as the repository of all truth, and in consequence dismiss all religious beliefs, simply because they are unscientific. Very often, this position is a reaction to disagreement in the religious sphere with apparently no agreed methods of resolving it. The idea is that science does not have this problem. Even if scientists are at odds with each other, they could, it is assumed, still agree on what would count as a proper scientific procedure, and proper scientific evidence. They know about how to go about resolving disputes, even if they do not immediately succeed.

Yet this is to play down the role of disagreement within science. Science would soon fossilize if everyone accepted the present state of science, and did not ask awkward questions about the basis of some theories. Scientific knowledge is at best partial, and must be open to challenge and revision. This normally takes place within an agreed framework of observation and experiment, but at the frontiers of science, such as in cosmology, the framework begins to break down. Theory then begins to outstrip our ability to check and test, and disagreement becomes more pronounced. Science itself begins to experience the difficulties faced by other bodies of belief. For example, many theoretical physicists are happy to talk of 'many universes'. Yet if universes are defined as inaccessible to each other—otherwise we would be merely referring to different regions of the same universe—science is dabbling in matters in which there can be no obvious procedure for resolving disputes. Our ability to know the truth becomes quickly separated from the issue of what the truth is. We are caught up in our limitations of space and time. Reality and our ability to know it are distinct. We cannot define what there is in terms of the methods of discovery which happen to be now available to us. Science and truth part company.

What do we do when we are confronted with scientists reaching out to a reality that eludes their grasp? The limitations of human reasoning become obvious. Do we dismiss such theories as a matter of faith, not reason? Do we, on the other hand, see that disagreement about truth does not necessarily mean that there is no truth? Science itself breeds radical disagreements, which threaten to transcend the settled procedures of established science. It can also elicit opposition to its purported monopoly of truth.

ATTACKS ON 'TRUTH'

In recent years, the 'modern' world, created by the Enlighten-ment in the eighteenth century, has been under attack, precisely because of its stress on the idea of a universal rationality, and a rationality moreover which finds its fruition in science, with its reliance on publicly accessible procedures. There has been a growing dissatisfaction with the claims of science, and other over-arching 'grand narratives', to sketch out what is universally true, according to rational principles which hold everywhere. So-called 'post-modernism' has often challenged the hegemony of science. Its protagonists have been impressed by the fact of diversity of belief, both through history and at any one time. They have recognized the existence of separate traditions of thought, each with their own standards of what is to count as true. Science is then not seen as the best exemplar of reason, let alone the only one. Instead it has to be put into context of time and place, and seen as a product of a particular historical period and culture. Religious believers have sometimes been tempted to seize gratefully on this understanding, as it appears to take the sting out of the scientific challenge to religion. If science is a cultural phenomenon, not a knowledge factory, it cannot afford to sit in judgement on religion, as non-rational, or even irrational. It cannot point to religious pluralism as some kind of fault, because it appears that scientific attitudes are merely another example of the plurality of beliefs that humans can take up quite arbitrarily. Certainly it is being denied that there is any overall rationality, shared by humans, which can lay hold of objective truth. All is conditioned by historical context.

This, however, is corrosive not just of scientific wishes to set epistemological standards; it removes any idea of objective truth. The reason that science cannot challenge religion is because, quite simply, it cannot claim truth. Yet this is not a point about science, but one about truth, saying it is relative to context. The result is that religion itself cannot aspire to truth, since all religions are themselves merely matters of transitory cultures. Religious practices can be said to be a part of human life, but they cannot be said to be about reality any more than science.

The wish to luxuriate in diversity, rather than to see it as a problem, is another prominent current in contemporary life. Not surprisingly, it is at odds with the pretensions of science. A desire to be tolerant, to live and let live, can seize gratefully on the idea that there can be no truth to fight for. The belief, however, that there are no facts—not even the fact of diversity of belief—can undermine itself very effectively. Why should we even be post-modernists, if there can be no reason to be? Why should we be concerned about diversity, when recognizing that there are different systems of belief, and different religions, appears to demand an ability to stand outside our own narrow context, and see things as they are? Many may instinctively draw back from the nihilism to which post-modernism inevitably draws us. For some though it appears to offer the opportunity of freedom. The Italian philosopher, Gianni Vattimo, for instance, explicitly links a belief in objective truth, and a 'real' world independent of our beliefs about it, with the abuse of authority and totalitarianism. He argues: 'If we accept the nihilistic destiny of our epoch and face the fact that we cannot rely upon any ultimate foundation, then any possible legitimation of the violent abuse of others vanishes'.[1] He claims that 'the real enemy of liberty is the person who thinks she can and should speak final and definitive truth'.[2] The problem is that he not only takes a stand against dogmatism, but also against the whole idea of truth. We are left with no resources for justifying the existence of individual freedom.

Perhaps even because of a generalized distrust of reason, some turn gratefully again to science, as a body of belief which can be trusted. They may accept the post-modernist analysis of non-scientific beliefs, but they try to retain a modernist approach to science. They are relativists about religion, thinking that different religions can be equally 'true for' their practitioners, but anti-relativist about science. The inherent tension in this is clear, but it is often encapsulated in the idea that science is objective, and deals with 'facts', in contrast with religion, which deals with subjective 'values'. The distinction carries with it echoes of the verificationism of the logical positivists between the two World Wars. They wanted to make truth dependent on our ability to test it through observation and experiment. Such verificationism has fallen on hard times, not least because theoretical physics wants itself to deal with theoretical entities which are unobservable. The attitude that lay behind verificationism, the respect for science, and the denigration of the non-scientific, still lives on. Labelling beliefs as 'values', and referring to 'value-judgements' may not say they are meaningless in so many words. The underlying idea is, though, that they are somehow found wanting in comparison with facts, because they cannot be checked and verified through scientific means. They are not part of the furniture of the world. The people holding values may be real, but the values themselves are, it seems, most certainly not. They are a matter for the individuals in question, not for public discussion. They are essentially matters of private concern.

Must We Privatize Religion?

Richard Rorty is an American philosopher who tries to combine a respect for science with an aggressive post-modernism. Science, he thinks, is acceptable in the public sphere, although it is none too clear why this should be, since, in his own words, 'we cannot regard truth as a goal of inquiry'.[3] Instead, in true pragmatist fashion, he believes that the purpose of inquiry 'is to achieve agreement among human beings about what to do'. Perhaps science may be able to bring this about in our time and place, but there is a question why. It may just be a matter of fashion, and fashions can change. Rorty, however, is convinced that science can be a matter for public discussion, and religion cannot be. He refers to 'the happy Jeffersonian compromise that the Enlightenment reached with the religious'. He explains that the compromise 'consists in privatising religion—keeping it out of... the public square'. Jefferson had famously referred to a 'wall of separation' between Church and State, but he used the phrase in a letter to Baptists who had theological concerns about an Established Church. In company with many others, Rorty transmutes the question about the relations between Church and Government into one about religion and society. Separating the latter two means driving religion from the public sphere. It has to become private, in the sense that individuals may espouse it, but it can no longer play a role in public discourse or public life.

In Rorty's words, 'the main reason religion needs to be privatized is that, in political discussion with those outside the relevant religious community, it is a conversation-stopper'.[4] He holds to the view of contemporary liberal philosophers that 'we shall not be able to keep a democratic political community going unless the religious believers remain willing to trade privatization for a guarantee of religious liberty'. In other words, they can be free to espouse religion as long as they keep quiet about it, and do not cause a public nuisance. The Enlightenment's legacy of distrust of religion, and of insulating it from the realm of reason, is held up as a good example. Rorty indeed describes 'the secularization of public life, as the Enlightenment's central achievement'. Yet since he also attacks the Enlightenment view that reason can transcend context, he manages simultaneously both to follow the Enlightenment and oppose it. There is no ground for privileging science, or down-grading religion, without a very particular doctrine about what counts as rational.

Rorty regards the stopping of conversation as the arbiter. The desirability of democratic agreement becomes the criterion. We are thus back with the idea that science has an agreed framework for discussion and settling disputes, while religion does not. Yet this only makes sense given some idea of a shared rationality into which science can tap, but religion cannot. What is it about science which makes it acceptable in the public sphere, and about religion which does not? Both will be equally acceptable to their adherents, if we adopt relativism. Something more than that will be needed to give an explanation why science should have such a privileged position. Only a metaphysical belief that what exists must be restricted to what is accessible to science can justify paying attention to science, and banishing religion from our public places. This begs the question against religion in a spectacular way. It is denigrated because it is based on metaphysics, and not empirical science. Yet the denigration itself depends on metaphysical assumptions.

The common reason for keeping religion from the public sphere is connected with Rorty's notion of it as a 'conversation-stopper'. Apart from underlying anti-religious assumptions, the contingent state of public opinion in contemporary societies is often invoked. We live, we are told, in pluralist societies, where radical disagreement is the norm in moral and religious matters, but not, it appears, in scientific ones. The only way, therefore, we can live together is by agreeing to differ on contentious matters, and keeping them 'private'. Rorty himself says firmly that 'the epistemic arena is a public space, a space from which religion can and should retreat'.[5]

The idea is that we need a liberal, democratic framework in which we can tolerate diversity. John Rawls is the political philosopher who has epitomized this approach. He says:

We must distinguish between a public basis of justification, generally acceptable to citizens on fundamental political questions, and the many non-public bases of justification—belonging to the many comprehensive doctrines, and acceptable only to those who affirm them.[6]

Once again, a distinction is introduced between public and private with religious views epitomizing the kind of view which has a 'non-public' basis of justification. Issues of justice and basic constitutional questions can only be resolved by appeal to what Rawls terms 'publicly shared methods of inquiry and forms of reasoning'.[7] He stresses 'the fact of reasonable pluralism', which he sees as the inevitable result of the 'powers of human reason at work within enduring, free, institutions'. There is thus always going to be disagreement about religion, and we have to agree a just framework, in which we can live together while still disagreeing. All this, under Rawls' scheme, takes place behind his 'veil of ignorance', where we do not know which views we will hold, or what place we will have, in the society. There is, accordingly, a pressure to be fair to everyone, without any inbuilt bias to some views.

This agreement, cannot, however, take place in a total vacuum, since it must itself have a rational basis. Rawls talks of shared methods of inquiry and forms of reasoning, assuming them 'to be familiar from common sense and to include the procedures and conclusions of science and social thought, where these are well established and not controversial'.[8] In other words, his just society assumes radical disagreement over religion, but takes the methods and conclusions of modern science as its starting point. Disagreements within science are deemed to be irrelevant. It follows that science can be taught in schools and religion cannot. Science is clearly assumed to be intrinsically less controversial than religion. It is in the public domain and religion is not.

Rawls is putting forward a political theory, not a metaphysical one, and it seems that he is advocating a framework which he thinks reflects current social reality. In Western societies people respect science but disagree about religion. Yet what justification is there for making a distinction? Rawls' dichotomy between public and private bases of justification depends on what is generally acceptable to citizens. Justification becomes just what happens to be accepted. On this understanding it seems as if religion and morality could be matters for public life, if we did not live in a 'pluralist' society, but one where there was a settled agreement on such matters. It all depends on what happens to be well established at any time in a given society. Yet what is generally acceptable? Only what people can agree about can be admitted to the public arena. Yet until there has been public debate, how does anyone know what in fact can command assent and what cannot?

TOLERATION AND TRUTH

There is need of a principled distinction between science and religion, rather than a mere appeal to current sociology. Why should democracy rely on science, but restrain the public parading of religion? We should move away from popular sociology about what is acceptable. Indeed the popularity of astrology might make us wonder how far even science is generally accepted. It is, though, remarkable that science converges on what is regarded as the truth. We tend to take it for granted that scientists agree, or at least agree on which procedures can produce agreement. Given enough information we expect convergence of belief. In contrast, it is assumed that not only does this not happen with religious belief, but in principle it could not.

One reason why scientists can be expected to agree, even if only at some hypothetical 'final agreement', is that they have something to agree about: namely the character of the physical world. That is the way the world is. This is the basic 'realist' understanding of science, which sees science as attempting to match our purported knowledge with an independent reality, which in turn constrains us. Pragmatists may wish to take the fact of agreement at face value, but this always leaves the more basic issue untouched of what justifies the agreement. When agreement alone is the aim, science quickly becomes a political matter requiring compromise, and give and take. It can no longer pretend to be a quest for truth, or the accumulation of knowledge.

The assumption that religious people have nothing to agree about only really becomes plausible when materialist, or atheist, assumptions are being smuggled in. The physical world, accessible to science, is then seen as comprising the whole of reality. Religion has nothing left in principle to appeal to in order to settle disputes. All we have are 'beliefs', with no fact of the matter to constrain them. While physical reality is seen as no figment of our imagination, but as something which can, and does, thwart us, God's objective reality is not taken seriously. Anyway, it will be said dismissively, it all depends which God. The possibility of any religious claims being true, in any but the most figurative sense, is not to be entertained. Pluralism is our starting point, and, religious disagreement becomes a further justification for relying on science alone.

Rawls linked pluralism to the operation of human rationality, given freedom. Yet science, as a rational process, is itself in a continually dynamic state, progressing through disagreement, and the testing of alternative theories. It depends on freedom, both on an individual and an institutional level, and has not progressed in some places and times, when the requisite freedom has been lacking. Totalitarian government stifles scientific inquiry. A uniformity of belief imposed on scientists for non-scientific reasons means the death of science. Without bold conjectures, and the stimulus of competing understandings, science will fossilize. Science can only progress given pluralism within it. Scientific theories must always be provisional, because our knowledge, if it is that, is still only partial. Everything has to be open to challenge and reassessment, and scientists must be open to ideas that challenge their assumptions. Knowledge can never expand if we become complacent and satisfied with what we think we already know. The expansion of knowledge thrives on the disagreement which occurs under conditions of freedom. Even science itself can be derided and rejected by some on the grounds that it is the source of many of the problems of modern life. In this respect, science, as a human practice, is not absolutely different from religion.

Some may retort that religion, unlike science, does not even aspire to form a unified body of knowledge. Even so, despite the differences between religions, a stress on the contrast between finite and infinite, the world around us and the transcendent, is sufficient to make any religious adherent acknowledge that our present knowledge can only be partial and provisional. Science and religion are both concerned with what may be true, and they both have to accept that human understanding will never be complete.

An authoritarian approach to religion can lay down what is and is not acceptable in a society, and individual freedom in religious matters can be ruled out. Yet just as science flourishes in an atmosphere of freedom, and depends on it, religion itself makes most sense when built on the idea of individual freedom. Certainly that is the import of the doctrine of human free will. The problem is that where there is freedom, there will be disagreement. Reality, however, does constrain us, so that there are limits to the beliefs which can be rationally held. Even so, under conditions of partial information and limited understanding, we may be handicapped. In science itself, the idea that we should be in possession of all relevant and possible empirical information seems purely hypothetical, except in very artificially constrained and limited cases.

'Pluralism' and divergence of belief are not a threat to the idea of truth. They are themselves part of science. It should not be surprising that religion finds the same, particularly when, by definition, it is dealing with matters that may well finally outstrip full human understanding. Both science and religion pre-suppose, and depend on, the freedom of individuals to form their own opinions and beliefs. Both need human rationality, and that itself requires a background of freedom. Someone who is coerced to believe something does not really believe it, but is only paying lip-service to it. The mindless imposition of religious orthodoxy may well be self-defeating, just as an imposition of scientific views goes against the very spirit of critical inquiry which should form the basis of science. This is an argument for religious toleration, but public toleration is very different from 'privatizing' religion. The latter makes religion such an individual matter, that it is not to be discussed in the public arena, let alone make any contribution in the formation of public policy. This makes sense once it seems that religion is not about anything at all, but is merely a matter of individual choice about how to live our lives. On the other hand, if religion appears to be making claims about an objective reality, this must have a universal significance. We all confront the same reality, and this should be a matter of public, as well as private, concern.

Disagreement is the life-blood of science, and the bed-rock of democracy. There is no need for democratic negotiation, or for politics at all, if everyone in a society is in perfect agreement. Insisting that disagreements are kept private, out of the public sphere, is to invite dishonesty. It encourages people to advocate policies for reasons that may not be their real reasons. Dishonesty and hypocrisy are, however, the least of it. There seems to be a fear of disagreements that we do not know how to solve. Yet this is the normal condition for citizens in a democracy, and indeed for humans in our life together. What is coyly called 'pluralism' is surely the common lot of humanity. Orthodoxy and uniformity are often enforced, precisely because they do not come naturally. We all have different understandings and commitments, but that does not mean that public reasoning cannot take account of them.

THE PUBLIC SPHERE

One of the problems is the slippery nature of the terms 'public' and 'private'. In one sense, religion is, and ought to be, a private matter. If we define 'public' as pertaining to the State (as when civil servants are regarded as 'public officials') then it is no part of the State's business what my religious beliefs are. They should in that sense be private. That is the relevance of the issues of compulsion and toleration, first dealt with by Locke. Yet in this sense, science should never be public either. If any government begins to require scientists to accept particular theories for the sake of political convenience, science is in big trouble, as indeed it has been under totalitarian regimes, such as that of the U.S.S.R. 'State science' must be a contradiction in terms, and although there have been, and are, many examples of 'State religion' in various forms, it runs the risk of being the antithesis of genuine religious commitment. Compulsory observance is not the same thing as worship freely given. Once there are publicly enforced standards in either science or religion, with government sanctions underwriting them, conformity rather than truth becomes the watchword.

Science must not be public in this sense, but it must be in the sense that its claims are publicly assessable. The positivists were right in seeing that public verification and falsification go to the heart of the scientific enterprise. Many scientific claims outstrip our ability to test them at any given time, but the purpose of science is to make claims which can be checked by anyone anywhere. Science can claim universality and objectivity, and that makes it irrelevant who is putting forward a particular scientific theory, or which continent they are in. Science is not a private matter, and a claim made in London can be tested in Beijing.

This is all common sense, in that the status of science in the public world is widely accepted. Science deals with matters of public relevance, or, at least, most people believe it does. Yet, again, this brings us back to the conundrum as to why science is publicly acceptable. It must be for a better reason than that people do accept it. If public reasons are merely what are taken to be acceptable at a given moment, that is a very insubstantial ground for refusing to allow some types of reason in the public sphere. Once we rule out the apparatus of an authoritarian State imposing a State religion, the question still remains why religious arguments cannot be heard in the 'public square', in the way scientific ones are. Excluding them seems equally authoritarian. Indeed if religion is deemed private, and science public, the very idea of rational dialogue between the two is ruled out. Reason is itself devalued.

The dichotomy between public and private does provide a means of removing religion from contact with science, let alone influencing it. Religion is restricted to those areas of personal life where it is believed that truth, a public concern, is not at stake. The corollary is that in religion there is nothing to discuss rationally. It dwells in areas public reason—and hence all reason—cannot reach. A further consequence of this is that science cannot be expected to teach religion anything. Both are insulated from each other.

Pluralism within science can be beneficial for its development. That suggests that, in society at large, the fact of competing beliefs does not necessarily suggest that truth is not at stake. Divergence of belief, as in science, should not turn us to a debilitating relativism, ruling out any idea of a shared rationality. It should rather be a spur for public, and rational, discussion. Disagreement within a democracy should be the prelude to more debate, not a withdrawal into ghettos. If we do not reach ready agreement, at least we may be able to understand each other's positions, and not hold them in contempt. The idea that any idea cannot be expressed and publicly discussed is a restriction on the very idea of democracy. There would be no need for democratic institutions if we all perfectly agreed all the time. Only if religious views are not regarded as being rationally held in the first place, could discussion be inappropriate. This is a convenient position for those who wish to marginalize religion. By appropriating for themselves or for science, the idea of rationality, religion can be seen as non-rational, if not irrational.

Democracy assumes the existence of varying viewpoints. As James Madison, later to be President of the United States, says in *The Federalist Papers* (debating the newly drafted Constitution of the United States): 'As long as the reason of man continues fallible and he is at liberty to exercise it, different opinions will be formed.'[9] The fact that conversations stop, and people cannot convince one another, does not mean that the issues are no longer of public concern. 'Public' reason cannot be limited to what is easily resolvable. Democracy itself cannot afford to shirk contentious and difficult matters. Pushed into the private sphere, they may continue to fester, with baleful consequences for the wider community.

The whole idea of the 'private' in the context of religion is rather curious. Religion is a private matter, in that it is a free personal choice, not dictated by the State. Political choices themselves, however, should be in that category, and that does not mean that they cannot be publicly discussed. The demands of freedom and those of rationality are intertwined. Human rationality cannot be parcelled up into self-contained compartments, let alone monopolized by some section. We all live in the same world, facing, in that sense, the same 'public', universal, objective reality. The project of privatizing religion means that religion cannot be concerned with any such public reality. Religion is prevented from making any public truth claims, or from being able to share in any overarching rationality. Thus a relativist view of truth in religion comes to prevail, coupled with a touching faith in science as the sole arbiter of objective truth. Yet allowing any relativism in any area is dangerous. Once part of human reasoning is enclosed in one compartment, the same considerations can lead to a distrust of all human reasoning. Post-modernism has no favourites, not even science.

A restriction on the idea of public reason, confining it to what is generally acceptable, prejudges democratic debate before it has even begun. We cannot be told what cannot be discussed. Rationality is not a political notion, and must not be defined too narrowly by science. It has to track the nature of the world. Human fallibility, and limited information, together mean that any restriction on what can be considered in the public arena has to arise from an unthinking dogmatism. The enemy of rational discussion is a misplaced certainty, and the arrogance which can arise from it. That is not the sole province of fundamentalist religion. Those who say that religion is a private matter are saying that a free society must tolerate it, but that religious claims contain nothing of substance, which can be publicly examined in a rational manner. That is a large claim, which would need considerable argument—itself the kind of argument which would have to take place in the public sphere.

On the other hand, many would say that religious claims are the most important of any that can be made about the world. They may all be false, but if any of them are true, they would under-pin our science, and our rationality. They would have to inform our politics. Defining public reason in such a way as not to allow such claims to be considered or their implications discussed, is, in fact, whether its proponents see it that way or not, a method of ensuring that, once a belief is classified as religious, it never gets the critical scrutiny it deserves.

11

Under God?

THE ESTABLISHMENT CLAUSE

ACCORDING TO the Bill of Rights, attached to the Constitution of the United States of America in 1789, 'Congress shall make no law respecting an establishment of religion, or prohibiting the free exercise thereof.' At a stroke, the separation of Church and State, and religious liberty, were made cornerstones of American life. Yet, at the same time, the United States is a very religious country, and religion is often publicly invoked. Coins proclaim 'In God We Trust', and the Pledge of Allegiance now refers to one nation 'under God'. From the beginning of the Republic, there were examples of official religious observance. Presidents proclaimed days of prayer. George Washington himself added the phrase 'so help me God' in taking the oath of office as President, with his hand on the Bible. Official chaplains are appointed to legislatures, a practice upheld in 1983, in a case concerning Nebraska. Abraham Lincoln's Gettysberg address included the words 'this nation under God shall have a new birth of freedom'. No contemporary inaugural address by a President is complete without biblical references and some invocation of God. The Senate Chamber in the State House in Boston has the words

'God Save the Commonwealth of Massachusetts' emblazoned at the front.

So one could go on, with numerous examples of the way in which religion is woven into the fabric of public life at federal and state levels. As Chief Justice Rehnquist pointed out in a judgement in 2004, even the Court Marshal's opening proclamation in the Supreme Court concludes with the words 'God save the United States and this honourable Court', a phrase which can be traced back to 1827.[1] The founders of the United States may have had their reasons for not having a religious establishment at federal level, but they did not think that they lived in a secular nation. As James Hitchcock comments: 'The Founders simply assumed the reality of a Christian nation, and thought that liberty was made possible through the discipline forged by religion.'[2] They certainly did not believe that religion was only a private matter. As Hitchcock sums up the situation:

The overall result was the emergence of what has been called a '*de facto* establishment' of a generalized kind of Protestantism that manifested itself in numerous public and official ways, a pattern present not only from the beginning of the Republic, but already part of the processes by which that Republic was called into being.[3]

An unfortunate aspect of this was a latent, and sometimes overt, anti-Catholicism, which was itself often the motive for the insistence on the separation of Church and State. Particularly after major immigration from Catholic countries, there was a fear of the influence of the Catholic hierarchy. The fear of Establishment had even deeper roots. It was often voiced by groups such as Baptists, who, like the Amish, believed that the people of God should be kept separate, and that Christ's kingdom had different purposes from that of the civil State.[4]

One such was Roger Williams, who was banished from Massachusetts in 1635, and went on to found 'Providence', Rhode Island. Meanwhile in Massachusetts, those who had rejected the Anglican Establishment in England went on to make a new one of their own. Congregationalism was in fact established in the state until 1833.

The very fact that Churches could be established in states decades after the adoption of the U.S. Constitution shows that the Establishment Clause was seen as applying only at federal level. Lingering distrust of the Church of England, coupled with denominational rivalry, led the Founders to be determined that the federal government should pursue a policy of neutrality concerning denominations. Yet there was another reason. James Madison, a significant figure in drawing up the Constitution, wrote in *The Federalist Papers* that it was important not only to guard against oppression by rulers, but 'to guard one part of the society against the injustice of the other part'.[5] There are, in other words, certain freedoms too precious to be at the mercy of majority vote. Madison argued that whilst all authority in the United States 'will be derived from and dependent on the society', the society will be broken up into so many interest groups that power can be diffused. He says:

> In a free government the security for civil rights must be the same as that for religious rights. It consists in the one case in the multiplicity of interests, and in the other in the multiplicity of sects.[6]

He was a leading opponent of Establishment, even in his home state of Virginia, where there had been an Anglican one.[7] There had been positive coercion, with legal penalties. We are told, in an example referred to in the present day Supreme Court, that in the Colony of Virginia:

Ministers were required by law to conform to the doctrines and rites of the Church of England; and all persons were required to attend church and observe the Sabbath, were tithed for the public support of Anglican ministers, and were taxed for the costs of building and repairing churches.[8]

With that historical background, it is hardly surprising that Madison saw the need for religious liberty.

Christian diversity, and squabbling between denominations, can be seen as a disadvantage. Madison, however, saw competition between sects as a guarantee that one would not try to dominate the others, and deprive them of rights. This has been the American way ever since, and some have attributed the vitality of American religion to the lack of Establishment. Yet there is no doubt that competition, and jealousy, between denominations has weakened their public witness. An opportunity has been given to those who want no place for religion at any official level.

What started as a separation of Church and State (or Jefferson's 'wall of separation') has become an attempt to separate religion from society. It is argued that all public recognition of religion is prohibited by the Establishment Clause. A significant step on this path was the agreement by the Supreme Court through the 1940s and 1950s that the Fourteenth Amendment's due process clause guaranteed personal liberties in the various states. Furthermore, such liberties were regarded as those defined by the Bill of Rights. The Establishment Clause, originally assumed to be inapplicable to states, came to be seen as a fundamental protection of religious liberty throughout the United States.

In the last fifty years, the Supreme Court has been progressively more rigorous about separating religion from public life.

Under God?

With its power to strike down legislation, the Court has not been afraid to take positions which went against public opinion, the decisions of Congress, and constitutional precedent. A cynic might wonder whether, in the case of religion, the judgements made have as much to do with the personalities and private beliefs of the nine justices as anything else. The appointment of justices to the Supreme Court has become a subject of major political controversy. Many believe that the President's ability, through careful nomination, to alter the character of the Court is amongst the most significant of his powers.

STATE SUPPORT OF RELIGION

Important principles were put forward by the U.S. Supreme Court in *Lemon v. Kurtzman* in 1971. The issue was the use of public money to subsidize private religious schools, even though this was for secular subjects, and not the teaching of religion. A standard was proposed with three parts, and this has subsequently become known as the *Lemon* test. It was said by the Court that a statute 'must have a secular legislative purpose', and that its primary effect 'must be one that neither inhibits nor advances religion'.[9] The third clause was that a statute must not foster 'an excessive entanglement with religion'. The *Lemon* test has tended to produce a separation of the whole apparatus of government and anything religious. Prayer and religious teaching is excluded from all public schools. Any financial help for religious organizations is *prima facie* unconstitutional. In 2002, a case allowing vouchers for attending a religious school opened the door again for some aid to religious institutions.[10] A cardinal principle, however, was that vouchers were given to individuals who exercised a choice about how to use them. Money did not go directly to religious institutions. The idea of giving financial help to 'faith-based communities' for social work is given impetus by the fact that in many American inner cities, the Churches and other religious organizations are the only institutions left who could conduct such work. The idea of money only being given for secular purposes will still be very prominent, but some will challenge such entanglement with religion.

The financing of religion by the State may appear as a mark of Establishment, but in Europe we have seen that the two do not necessarily go together. The Supreme Court's reluctance to allow public money to be used for such a purpose is understandable, given American history. However, the Establishment Clause is only part of the story, since the Constitution also guarantees the 'free exercise' of religion. In 2003, in *Locke v. Davey*,[11] the Supreme Court dealt with a case in which a student from the State of Washington was stopped from using a scholarship for academically gifted students from the State to study for a 'pastoral ministries' degree, which the Court described as 'devotional'.[12] The Washington Constitution forbade public money being applied to any 'religious worship, exercise or instruction'. The question was whether the student's right to practise his religion was being denied. The Court did not agree that it was, since the state's interest in not funding devotional degrees was substantial. It held that the Establishment Clause and the Free Exercise Clause 'are frequently in tension', and went on to remark that it has long said that 'there is room for play in the joints between them'.[13]

This decision, however, raises questions. No one denomination or religion was being favoured, since no scholarship can be used for any theological training. As Justice Scalia pointed out in his Dissent, the fact remains that a generally available public benefit has been withheld in one area alone, namely religion.[14] It seems that any public programme could exclude religion. Equality of treatment, and freedom from discrimination are considered less important than the pressing need for the State to keep its distance from religion. Justice Scalia asks rhetorically 'What next? Will we deny priests and nuns their prescription-drug benefits on the ground that tax-payers' freedom of conscience forbids medicating the clergy at public expense?'[15] As he says, public benefits which are made generally available become 'part of the baseline against which burdens on religion are measured'.[16] He believes that when the State 'withholds that benefit from some individuals solely on the basis of religion, it violates the Free Exercise Clause no less than if it had imposed a special tax'. The Court as a whole, however, did not agree that an undue burden had been placed.

Although public bodies in the United States fear 'entanglement' with religion, the requirement that secular purposes be paramount implies an ability to distinguish between the secular and religious in both general and particular cases. Yet that involves an investigation which might involve judgements, which could impinge on theology in a manner that produces 'entanglement'. One form of neutrality could be, in the case of scholarships, to treat all religiously affiliated Colleges equally, and on a par with non-religious ones. All that would matter was that the College was duly accredited, not what subject was being studied in it. Current Supreme Court thinking, however, seems to think that equal treatment of that kind is not neutral enough. The State should have nothing to do with religion. In other words, the neutrality advocated is vaguely antagonistic to religion rather than supportive of it. Public life, it seems, has to be kept rigidly apart from any religious involvement.

THE PLEDGE OF ALLEGIANCE

Rituals and symbols can have a powerful influence and the U.S. Supreme Court has been particularly concerned with possible effects of coercion in these matters on children and young people. Having to hear the Bible read, or to participate in public prayer, is thought to be in that category. The right of withdrawal from anything religious might appear to safeguard individual freedom, but the Court has been concerned about the effects of peer pressure. There might be an ensuing impression that those who do not wish to conform to a general practice are in some sense not behaving as citizens should. Yet it could be argued on the other side that children are being educated to think that belief in God is irrelevant to being a citizen and is entirely an optional extra, according to taste. The absence of a practice, as much as its presence, undeniably gives a message.

In the United States, schoolchildren are expected to recite a Pledge of Allegiance to the flag each day, with a right for students to abstain, if, like Jehovah's Witnesses, they have objections. The current text of the Pledge is:

I pledge allegiance to the Flag of the United States of America, and to the Republic for which it stands, one nation under God, indivisible, with Liberty and Justice for all.[17]

Under God?

The words 'under God' were added in 1954, in the face of the perceived threat of Communism, and the Pledge raises important issues about the relation of American society to religion. The reference to 'God' in this context, can include any monotheistic religion, but it certainly appears to rule out atheism. The reciting of the Pledge has been challenged by a self-confessed atheist, Michael Newdow, who argued that it constituted religious indoctrination of his daughter.[18] It would thus both contravene the Establishment Clause, and the Free Exercise Clause. The facts of the particular case allowed the Court to side-step what was a politically controversial issue. They were able to rule that Newdow had no standing to bring the case, as he was separated from the child's mother, who in any case wanted a religious education for the girl. The substantive issue therefore still remained to be decided.

The issue is a tricky one for the Supreme Court. Its own reasoning about 'entanglement' with religion might suggest that the Pledge was unconstitutional, because it looks as if it is endorsing a belief in God. It has previously even ruled out prayer at a graduation ceremony, although attendance was voluntary.[19] Yet public opinion was opposed to changing the Pledge, as was Congress. The Court's general stance is illustrated by Justice O'Connor. In concurring with the Court's decision, she reiterates opposition to any identification of the State with any religious views. In particular, she applies 'the endorsement test'. She holds that 'government must not make a religious belief relevant to his or her standing in the political community by conveying a message that religion or a particular religious belief is favored or preferred'.[20] Endorsing a religion, she believes, 'sends a message to non-adherents that they are outsiders, not full members of the political community, and an accompanying message to adherents that they are insiders, favored members of political community'.[21]

This is a core argument in a pluralist society for isolating religion. It is hard, though, to see any official policy as so uncontroversial that a message is not sent to some that they are in a minority, and, on this reasoning, an 'outsider'. Some people may feel excluded when they cannot get their way, but that is the nature of democracy. There will be minorities, and their rights must be protected. O'Connor, however, seems to go further. The United States should not appear to give even a hint of an endorsement of religion. Yet, as we have constantly seen, what has been termed 'the naked public square', denuded of the trappings of religion, can itself constitute an onslaught on religious liberty. Believers are restrained from acknowledging and expressing their faith in public. When the traditions of a country have in this way been directly challenged, many see the State as becoming actively hostile to religion.

If a country is not allowed to endorse religion, it is saying that its basic principles of justice are independent of religion. Valuing individual citizens, cherishing their rights, upholding equality and the ideals of democracy, all have secular sources. They have no need of religious education to support them. Many may think this. Nevertheless, the United States was, as a matter of historical fact, founded on a religious basis, and its earliest settlers had left their own land for religious reasons. It is therefore a striking position for the U.S. Supreme Court to adopt.

One might think, as a consequence, that Justice O'Connor would find the phrase 'under God' inappropriate in the Pledge. She argues that although there may be similar uses of religious language in public life, 'they are more properly understood as employing the idiom for essentially secular purposes'.[22] For example, 'they commemorate the role of religion in our history'. Such references to God belong to a category called by O'Connor 'ceremonial deism'.[23] In a move hardly likely to appeal to believers, she suggests that the phrase 'under God' does not mean what it appears to, and has no necessary religious connotation. She does, however, say:

> Even if taken literally, the phrase is merely descriptive; it purports only to identify the United States as a Nation subject to divine authority. That cannot be seen as a serious invocation of God, or as an expression of individual submission to divine authority.[24]

Yet to say that the United States, like other nations, is under divine authority is to make a substantial and sobering claim. It cannot be dismissed as being merely ceremonial. O'Connor seems so to concentrate on the private side of religious commitment, that she fails to see the importance of an admission that nations too are guided by God. The argument about religion in public life is often precisely about that issue. There is also the question as to whether basic ideals of freedom and equality are robust enough to stand alone. O'Connor herself refers to the 'religious history that gave birth to our founding principles of liberty'.[25] She comments that 'it would be ironic indeed if this Court were to wield our constitutional commitment to religious freedom so as to sever our ties to the traditions developed to honor it'.

The problem is that if traditions have given rise to beliefs about liberty, this may be more than an interesting historical accident. The traditions may actually help to sustain the belief, and be necessary for the principles to survive and be transmitted to future generations. O'Connor has implicitly posed the question how far a country can derive its principles from religious tradition, and then use those principles to distance itself from that tradition. 'Ceremonial deism' may be more important than O'Connor implies. Chief Justice Rehnquist in his judgement on the same case, sees the Pledge as in no sense a religious exercise, but a simple recognition of the fact that the United States 'was founded on a fundamental belief in God'.[26] That may be so, but any official refusal to continue to acknowledge that fact must involve a significant change in the Nation's outlook.

The idea of 'ceremonial deism' accepts religious utterances on occasion in the public sphere, but empties them of any content. This may square a circle from a legal point of view. It allows time-honoured references to God. Yet, through the U.S. Supreme Court's modern understanding of the Establishment Clause, it can still deny there is any contact between religion and the State. However, the ubiquitous references to God and religion, entwined with American public life, suggest that the Supreme Court's recent understanding is at odds with the Founders' intentions, and with the traditions of the United States ever since. That would not worry those legal theorists, who think that a Court cannot be bound by the intentions of the writers of a constitutional text in very different social conditions. Yet all kinds of social and political pressures can then influence judges. Their decisions can become unpredictable, and even at times inconsistent. The law itself becomes an instrument of other interests.

FREE EXERCISE?

One consequence of the idea that the State must not endorse any form of belief is its refusal to become involved in questions about truth. The fear of 'entanglement' stems from a desire not to become involved in complicated, and divisive, theological controversy. In a democratic society, the mere fact that people hold beliefs is enough. On this assumption, it cannot align itself with Christian belief, but at the same time cannot imply that it is false. Official neutrality will become tantamount to saying that it does not matter whether Christianity is true or false. This sits well with the more sophisticated view that religion is a matter of 'faith', not reason, so that all beliefs must be respected, whatever their content. The problem for the Supreme Court is how to adopt an even-handed approach to all types of religion, without retreating into relativism. In practice, the Court has had to draw the line somewhere, as with the issue of polygamy. Yet the protection of religion under the Free Exercise Clause does give it privileges, and even immunity from the criminal law. The Supreme Court made it clear in 2006 that the *Religious Freedom Restoration Act* of 1993 stopped the Federal Government from 'substantially burdening' a person's exercise of religion, without a 'compelling interest'.[27] Thus even prohibited drugs can be used in religious ceremonies. Members of every recognized Indian tribe are exempted from the ban on peyote, and in the 2006 case a religious sect, with origins in the Amazon Rainforest, was allowed to use a sacramental tea containing a banned hallucinogen. The Court held that the sect's 'sincere religious practice' should be accommodated.[28]

Sincerity of belief, rather than reasons which stand up to public scrutiny, become the benchmark for dealing with religion. As one writer on the decisions of the U.S. Supreme Court puts it: 'Religion is not treated as real in the way that believers regard it as real, and the irreducible mysteriousness of religion leads the Court to define it as irrational, private and divisive.'[29] Presumably the reality of religion referred to is a belief in an objective reality, such as that of God. The Court, on the other hand, would see the only reality in religion as being the fact of beliefs being 'really' and 'sincerely' held. They can cope with religious belief as a psychological fact, and a social reality, but not as a claim to truth. For many years the Court has taken the explicit line that religion was a personal, subjective affair, not subject to rational constraints, or open to public debate. As long ago as the *Ballard* case of 1944, the majority opinion held that Americans were free to believe what they wanted, and did not have to prove beliefs, which might be incredible to others.[30]

What begins with a respect for liberty passes to a gradual forging of the links between privacy, subjectivity, and irrationality. Religion cannot aspire to 'public reason'. This has the effect of making other people's reactions to religious belief important. From the viewpoint of public policy, it is as significant if people take offence at public displays of religion, or social practices, as if people wish to practise their religion. The one has to be balanced against the other. When, in addition, the protection of minorities is a priority, the feelings of alienation and offence of a small number of people will more than balance the wishes of the majority for public recognition of their faith.

Issues about religious freedom should not rely on the protection of sensitivities, which are always difficult to define. When the law is invoked, it should deal with actual coercion, and genuine limitations on freedom. Thus in the Pledge case, it is important that reciting the Pledge is voluntary. As Justice Thomas points out, 'the traditional "establishments of religion" to which the Establishment Clause is addressed necessarily involve actual legal coercion'.[31] The United States, at least at federal level, set itself from the beginning against any compulsion to conform to religious demands. Article VI of the Constitution also requires that there be no religious test for the holding of office. It also allows for all elected representatives and for specified officials to be bound to the Constitution 'by Oath or Affirmation'. No-one could be coerced into giving a religious oath, but at the same time those who wished could do so. Thus there was even in that trivial instance recognition of the importance of religion, without coercion. In the same way, the mere existence of the Free Exercise Clause in the Bill of Rights could be seen as identifying religion as so important that it has to be given special protection. So far from inhibiting public recognition, it itself constitutes it. As Hitchcock comments: 'By the very enactment of the Free Exercise Clause, the Framers in effect "established" religion by giving it special protection.'[32] There is in fact a tension in the attitude of the Supreme Court between its efforts to remove signs of public recognition of religion, and the way it publicly protects some religion from criminal laws which are supposed to apply to everyone.

DISPLAYING THE TEN COMMANDMENTS

In the United States all forms of public manifestation of religion are likely to be the subject of legal challenge, if a public authority appears to endorse it. Even the public display of symbols becomes controversial. There has been agitation for the removal of displays of the Ten Commandments in public places. Some of them enjoin particular religious beliefs and practices, such as keeping the Sabbath, but others would appear to many to be the bedrock of society. A State that wishes to be neutral about the desirability of murder is getting itself into a curious position. Presumably, though, the basic objection is that they are said to be commandments of God, and so displaying them might imply an acceptance of the idea of God. An atheist State may wish to keep well clear of them. A Christian, or Jewish, State would give them prominence. The issue of their display once again raises in concrete fashion whether there is, or ought to be, any middle ground between appearing to advocate a broadly based religious view, or being put in the same position as an atheist State.

The Ten Commandments cannot be displayed in an American public school. There are, however, many instances of monuments setting out the Commandments being erected over the years in public places such as parks. For example, a five-foot high granite monument was set up by the Fraternal Order of Eagles in 1965 in a public park in Plattsmouth, south of Omaha in Nebraska. The problem is that the park and monument is owned by the City of Plattsmouth. A case was first brought in 2001 by an anonymous citizen 'John Doe'. In the words of the judgement for the United States Court of Appeals Eighth Circuit, he 'is an atheist and as such does not share the religious beliefs expressed on the monument'.[33] The key point is that 'the monument alienates Doe and makes him feel like a second-class citizen'. The divisiveness of any public endorsement of religion is thus invoked. Doe must be a very sensitive soul, since the letters on the monument are too small to be read from the street as he drives by. Nevertheless Doe knows it is there.

The Court then applied the *Lemon* tests, and could find no evidence of secular purpose. It comments that 'it is one thing for Plattsmouth to say one should not steal: it is quite another for Plattsmouth to say there is a God who said "Thou shalt not steal".[34] Many over the centuries, including Locke, have thought a religious backing for morality might be more effective than platitudes from Plattsmouth. That, though, was not the view of the Court, which was that 'the state may not express an opinion about religious matters' nor 'encourage citizens to hold certain religious beliefs'.[35] The Court also maintained that the effect of having the monument was religious and not secular. It says that 'the reasonable viewer would perceive this monument as an attempt by Plattsmouth to steer its citizens in the direction of mainstream Judeo-Christian religion'. The Court ruled that 'this it cannot do'.

After this decision, consideration of the legality of similar monuments was given by the Supreme Court, and in the light of one of their decisions, the Eighth Circuit, sitting en banc (with all the judges of the Circuit) in a rehearing reversed the decision. Their reasoning was that 'like the monument at issue in *Van Orden*, the Ten Commandments monument installed in Memorial Park by the City of Plattsmouth is a passive acknowledgment of the roles of God and religion in our nation's history'.[36] The Ten Commandments certainly influenced the development of America and its laws, but, to an extent, this is to dodge a more fundamental issue. How far can the United States afford, in its public life, to treat the religious traditions of the country as mere quaint survivals? Two Circuit judges dissented from the judgement, and claimed that 'to say that a monument inscribed with the Ten Commandments is nothing more than an "acknowledgment of the role of religion" diminishes their sanctity to believers and belies the words themselves'.[37] They would therefore still forbid the public display of the monument, so as to separate religion from public life. Another reaction, however, might be to say that the Ten Commandments mean what they say, but that is no reason for not accepting that there is public place for them, even if they do not represent the beliefs of all citizens. The fact that they are valued by many ought to be significant, and it was no doubt in that spirit that the original gift of the monument was accepted.

Of the two cases which the Supreme Court considered in 2005, one was from Kentucky, (*McCreary County v. A.C.L.U.*) where the Ten Commandments had been officially displayed in two courthouses, latterly as part of a more general exhibit. The other was the one referred to by the Eighth Circuit, *Van Orden v. Perry,* where a six foot high monolith, inscribed with the Ten Commandments, was one of many historical monuments in the grounds surrounding the State Capitol. One again it was a gift from the Fraternal Order of Eagles. Matters were hardly clarified, however, when the Court allowed the Texas monument, but ruled against the Kentucky displays. Both judgements revealed deep divisions in the Court, extending even to the role of the Court in interpreting the Constitution, and the meaning of democracy. Each case was decided five to four, with one judge switching sides. In so far as a rationale for the different decisions could be ascertained, the Texas display served a primarily non-religious purpose, and had been unchallenged for fifty years. The Kentucky display, however, was within the courthouse, and deemed to have a primarily religious purpose. Applying *Lemon*, it was therefore inadmissible.

Arguments about monuments, sometimes in inconspicuous positions, may seem trivial. The arguments about them, however, are surrogates for the question how far God should be publicly acknowledged in the United States. The Ten

Commandments arouse particular passions, because they symbolize the dependence of human law on the divine will. In fact the Chief Justice poses the dilemma when he says: 'Our institutions presuppose a Supreme Being, yet these institutions must not press religious observances upon their citizens.'[38] He later comments that 'recognition of the role of God in our Nation's heritage has also been reflected in our decisions'.[39] Yet these issues are precisely what are being fought over. Many see the separation of Church and State as implying that the United States must be an avowedly secular country.

Public opinion in the United States is overwhelmingly in support of public recognition of religion. Votes in Congress and in the various states reflect that. This means that, although the courts may wish to protect minorities, the question arises of the function of a Supreme Court in a democracy. Just because freedom is important, there has to be a limit to how far the wishes of an overwhelming majority can be deliberately ignored. The Court is only justified in ignoring them if it can appeal to a clear legal principle. It may for instance wish to prevent the unjust coercion of individuals to act against their consciences. Justice Scalia points out in his dissent in the Kentucky case that 'what distinguishes the rule of law from a shifting Supreme Court majority is the absolutely indispensable requirement that judicial opinions be grounded in consistently applied principle'.[40]

What principles are being invoked in these cases? The Opinion of the Court in the Kentucky case says crisply: 'The touchstone for our analysis is the principle that the First Amendment mandates governmental neutrality between religion and religion, and between religion and non-religion.'[41] Yet this hardly sits well with the Chief Justices's view that

American institutions presuppose a Supreme Being. Justice O'Connor is particularly concerned about the alleged divisiveness of religion, and claims: 'Allowing government to be a potential mouthpiece for competing religious ideas risks the sort of division that might easily spill into suppression of rival belief'.[42] She asserts that 'tying secular and religious authority together poses risks to both'. That may be an argument against too close an identification. Yet the question must be the deeper one of the source of authority. To say that 'the people' are the ultimate source of authority and law is to deny the 'truths' expressed in the Declaration of Independence 'that all men are created equal; that they are endowed by their Creator with certain unalienable rights'.

In the eyes of many, religion is the main influence on the United States and its ideas. This was the view of the French observer of American life in the early nineteenth century, Alexis de Tocqueville. He observed that 'the Americans combine the notions of Christianity and of liberty so intimately in their minds that it is impossible to make them conceive of one without the other'.[43] He claimed that religion was even more necessary in a democratic republic than elsewhere. Without a strong authority over them, citizens would need to have strong characters derived from strong principles. He asks rhetorically:

How is it possible that society should escape destruction if the moral tie is not strengthened in proportion as the political tie is relaxed? And what can be done with a people who are their own masters if they are not submissive to the deity?

Sentiments like these have led to the display of the Ten Commandments. Yet current Court doctrine outlaws religious motivation for public actions. A footnote to the Opinion of the

Court in the Kentucky case, concerning *McCreary County*, accepts that at least since 1947, 'it has been clear that Establishment Clause doctrine lacks the comfort of categorical absolutes'.[44] In other words there has been no consistency in the Court's decisions. One underlying problem is that the doctrine of neutrality collided with the democratically expressed wishes of the people. It is ironic that the pursuit of neutrality to religion has been itself the source of much division in American society.

The relevant issue is not what the government says, nor even the historical assumptions of institutions. The question is whether a government, and legal system, are to coerce citizens. There is no suggestion that, in the United States, Americans who do not respect the Ten Commandments, nor believe in God, suffer any disadvantage. Certainly there are no legal penalties threatening them. The most that they can appeal to are hurt feelings. Justice Thomas suggests in concurring with the judgement on *Van Orden* that the prevailing confusion could be removed 'if the Court would return to the views of the Framers (of the Constitution) and adopt coercion as the touchstone for our Establishment Clause inquiry'. As things stand, it could be argued that the opinions of minorities are severely restricting the religious freedom of the majority in the United States.

Conclusion

THE ILLUSION OF NEUTRALITY

THE LAW of European countries, and of others such as Canada and the United States, has to face the problems of a pluralist society. In a democracy, it might seem that the will of the majority should prevail, but that can well result in unfair treatment to minorities, who want equal recognition as citizens of their country. That has resulted in the contemporary stress on human rights, which provide protection against the tyranny of a majority. Religious liberty has always been seen as one of the most prominent of those rights, going to the heart of what it is to be a human being, able to choose what kind of life to live. Appeals to such rights are now of central importance in many jurisdictions.

The United States, with its separation of Church and State, has always tried to accommodate differences in religion, although originally this meant refusing to favour one particular Protestant denomination. It may seem a simple matter to offer religious freedom, but the question then arises as to the role of the State in doing so. Does this imply that the apparatus of government must be neutral between all forms of belief, and between belief and unbelief? That is the French position, with its policy of *laïcité*. It is also a position which is being increasingly advocated in the United States, and also passionately opposed.

For example, in the U.S. Supreme Court, Justice Stevens has argued that the government 'must remain neutral between valid systems of belief'.[1] He accepts that the American position started out as the view that there should be no discrimination between different Christian sects but he goes on to claim: 'As religious pluralism has expanded, so has our acceptance of what constitutes valid belief systems.' He sees 'the evil of discriminating today against atheists, polytheists, and believers in unconcerned deities' as 'the direct descendant of the evil of discriminating among Christian sects'. There thus appears to be no limit to what kind of belief system is 'valid'. It is equally valid to deny the existence of God or to affirm it, to say there are many gods or one, or to say that God loves us, or is unconcerned about us. Yet all of these statements cannot be true at once in any objective sense of truth. 'Validity' is clearly viewed as something different. Contradictions do not matter. Presumably all that is needed for a belief's validity is for it to be held sincerely. Yet for validity to depend on a belief's being held is a form of relativism. Validity then merely means that beliefs seem valid to those that hold them.

Positions like this seem to express tolerance while giving no reason to be tolerant. Forbidding public recognition of beliefs means that they cannot be rationally discussed. Yet rationality is something we all hold in common as humans. If public reasoning can have no relevance to religion, or equivalent systems of belief, we are restricting the scope of what may help us to understand each other more, even if it does not always bring agreement. In fact, relativism, the opponent of such rationality, always sinks into incoherence, by having in the end to assume something as true. When Justice Stevens talks of the 'evil' of discriminating between systems of belief, where is he standing to make that judgement about evil? He clearly has a system of belief himself, encompassing toleration of all belief, and he considers it important enough to impose it in others using the full force of law.

Justice Stevens says very clearly that 'the principle that guides my analysis is neutrality'.[2] In other words, 'the government must remain neutral between religion and irreligion'.[3] He recognizes that this would have seemed foreign to some of the Framers of the U.S. Constitution. If one regards any constitution as a 'living tree', to be interpreted and changed to fit the understandings (and prejudices) of the present age, that may not seem to matter. Yet the idea that it is possible to be neutral about religion is illusory. Either religion is of central importance for public life or it is not. Those who advocate neutrality are in effect saying that religion is a matter for individual decision, and must not seek or gain any form of public recognition. That may seem to allow for religious freedom, but it actually restricts the scope of religion in a controversial way.

IS THE STATE SELF-SUFFICIENT?

The removal of public recognition of religion in the United States and elsewhere, proclaims the self-sufficiency of the State. Modern democratic theory is reluctant to see the sphere of collective agreement and common action as having any foundation beyond itself. Even in the sphere of law, the temptation is to regard constitutional texts less as constraints on contemporary practice than as malleable instruments to be fashioned according to the demands of the day. The U.S. Bill of Rights dates from 1789, but in the case of the Canadian *Charter of Rights and Freedoms*, dating from 1982, the process of reinterpretation has already begun. Traditional law is often moulded to fit the contemporary world, rather than the other way round. It is hardly surprising that nations are even more reluctant to see their actions as circumscribed by obligations to some transcendental realm.

The urge to privatize all faith may have deeper roots than a desire to be fair to all citizens. It may also stem from a reluctance to admit that the State is subject to any higher authority than itself. Even if the State is seen as merely the artefact of the will of the people, the idea that there are no constraints on that will is dangerous. The doctrine of human rights, however, assumes that this is wrong, that there are objective standards which whole States can trample on, and be judged wrong in doing so. A right such as freedom of religion, and the connected right to practise it, is of universal application. Those who, for example, do not allow their citizens to change their religion are rightly condemned. The apparatus of human rights can be seen as an application of more general principles of natural law, connecting rights with ideas of what it is to be properly human, and to flourish as a human should.

Countries which have seen, and still see, themselves as built on a Christian basis see their authority as not only derived from a transcendental origin, but also as essentially constrained because of that. Even if democratic principle says that the fundamental requirement is the consent of the people, there is still the issue of what that consent must be based on. It cannot be arbitrary, but should itself be rationally grounded. If all reasoning on the public stage has to be purged of religious influence, the very idea of a religious basis for the State, and for political authority, is summarily dismissed. That may sit well with agnostic and atheist beliefs, but it is opposed to any traditional religious understanding of the need for those in government, and for those electing them, to be restrained by realizing their own reliance on a higher authority. The idea that even the powerful will be called to account for their actions before the throne of God can be a salutary check on abuses of power. The separation of religion, and religious forms of reasoning, from any relevance to public life is far from neutral in its effects. Qualities such as a respect for human dignity and human liberty have to be fostered and passed on to future generations. They do not flourish in a philosophical vacuum, but need proper grounding.

A COMMON RATIONALITY

Some forms of religion can give rise to intolerance and cruelty. Some are downright irrational. In the West, Christianity has for centuries provided the motive force behind the urge to value our common humanity, and to cherish individual liberty. Even if some dispute this, the fact that it is arguable should be enough to give religion a place in the public sphere, in order to make its claims. Those who see some religions as dangerous should acknowledge that pushing religion into the dark recesses of private life merely shields it all from public scrutiny and criticism.

Suggesting that reasons grounded in religion should not be advanced on the public stage merely protects religion, and the public behaviour inevitably flowing from it, from public scrutiny and rational debate. The only ground for considering religion to be beyond the reach of public reasoning is if no religion is in the business of reason. Either reason is then being defined too narrowly so as, say, only to encompass scientific reasoning, or it is thought that religion is of no public concern because it cannot claim truth. Yet keeping religion out of public discussions because it is not true is to beg a very large question.

The issue in a pluralist society should not be the need for a State's neutrality between all possible views. That is impossible. What is important is that its laws respect the basic principle of religious liberty and tolerate diversity. The institutions of the State do not have to be purged of religious influence, to allow those who are at odds with the heritage of a particular country to live in freedom within it. It is a paradox in contemporary England that the Establishment of the Church of England is often seen even by non-Christian faiths not so much as imposing a particular religion on anyone but as providing an umbrella under which those other faiths can shelter in order to obtain public recognition. So far from religion being regarded as a private matter, religion as such can be seen as having a contribution to make to the political process. Its voice, or voices, are heard, even if they do not necessarily carry the day.

The opposite path is for the State to proclaim its refusal to pay attention to any form of religious belief, while allowing it to be practised in private. Yet the path from official neutrality to indifference, and then hostility, to religion can be surprisingly short. Governments have to understand why religious liberty matters, and whether all religions should be treated equally. Once one asks such questions, issues of truth arise. Everyone's beliefs cannot be true, and although the right to hold apparently mistaken views is a precious one, any country still has to be guided by principles. Public debate about the proper basis for society is necessary, and religious voices should be heard in that debate. Religion has not just been one of the most formative influences on human society; religions make claims, which, if true, would be of universal importance. Religious voices must be heard in the public life of every country.

Notes

Introduction

1. Roger Trigg, *Rationality and Religion*, Blackwell, Oxford, 1998
2. Roger Trigg, *Rationality and Science*, Blackwell, Oxford, 1993
3. Roger Trigg, *Morality Matters*, Blackwell, Oxford, 2005
4. *Kitzmiller v. Dover Area School District*, U.S. District Court, Middle District of Pennsylvania, Case 04cv2688, Memorandum Opinion, December 20th 2005, p.28
5. *Kitzmiller*, p.31
6. *Kitzmiller*, p.66
7. *Kitzmiller*, p.65
8. *Kitzmiller*, p.64

Chapter 1

1. Silvio Ferrari and W. Cole Durham Jr. (eds), *Law and Religion in Post-Communist Europe*, Peeters, Leuven, 2003, 'Church and State in the Czech Republic', Jiri Rajmund Tretera, p.88
2. Ferrari, p.82
3. Ferrari, 'Church and State in Hungary', Balazs Schanda, p.123
4. Ferrari, 'Church and State in Latvia', Ringolds Balodis, p.148
5. Ferrari, 'Church and State in Slovenia', Lovro Sturm

6. Ferrari, 'Church and State in Russia', Lev Simkin, p.261
7. Ferrari, 'Religious Freedom', Giovanni Barberini, p.11
8. Ferrari, 'Law and Church-State Relations in Russia', Vsevolod Chaplin
9. Ferrari, 'Church and State in Slovakia', Peter Mulik, p.322
10. Ferrari, p.324
11. Charles Taylor, *Modern Social Imageries*, Duke University Press, Durham, NC, 2004, p.87
12. Taylor, p.89
13. Taylor, p.93
14. Elmer John Thiessen, *In Defence of Religious Schools and Colleges*, McGill-Queen's University Press, 2001, p.140
15. John Locke, 'An Essay on Toleration', *Political Essays*, ed. Mark Goldie, p.154, Cambridge University Press, Cambridge, 1997
16. *Select Committee Report on Religious Offences in England and Wales*, House of Lords, 2002–3, p.38
17. *Select Committee*, p.13
18. D. Fergusson, *Church State and Civil Society*, Cambridge University Press, Cambridge, 2004, p.186
19. Fergusson, p.194
20. Fergusson, p.193
21. Fergusson, p.194
22. Fergusson, p.187
23. Robert Audi, *Religious Commitment and Secular Reason*, Cambridge University Press, Cambridge, 2000, p.37
24. Audi, p.36

CHAPTER 2

1. Robert Audi, Religious Commitment and Secular Reason, Cambridge University Press, Cambridge, 2000, p.38

2. See, for instance, M. Scalabrino (ed.), *International Code on Religious Freedom*, Peeters, Leuven, 2003, p.153

3. Audi, p.4

4. Gianni Vattimo, *Nihilism and Emancipation*, Columbia University Press, New York, 2004, p.98

5. Vattimo, p.98

6. Audi, p.89

7. Audi, p.86

8. See my *Morality Matters*, Blackwell, Oxford, 2005

9. Audi, p.96

10. Audi, p.96

11. This was Habermas' argument in his lecture on 'Religion in the Public Sphere', University of London, July 1st 2005

12. J. Habermas, *Religion and Rationality*, Polity Press, Cambridge, 2002, p.150

13. Habermas, p.151

14. See my *Reason and Commitment*, Cambridge University Press, Cambridge 1973, p.14ff

15. *Explanatory Notes to Racial and Religious Hatred Bill*, introduced to House of Commons, 9th June 2005

16. *Guidelines for Review of Legislation Pertaining to Religion or Belief*, OSCE p.8, adopted by Venice Commission 2004

17. *Remmers v. Brewer* 494 F.2d 11277 (8th Circuit 1974)

CHAPTER 3

1. See M. Scalabrino (ed.), *International Code on Religious Freedom*, Peeters, Leuven, 2003, p.391

2. Preface to *International Code* by A. A. Cancado Trinidade, p.XI

3. J. Hitchcock, *The Supreme Court and Religion in American Life*, Vol I, Princeton University Press, Princeton, NJ, 2004, p.24
4. Hitchcock. Vol I, p.24
5. Peggy DesAutels, Margaret P. Battin, Larry May, *Praying for a Cure*, Rowman and Littlefield, Lanham, MD, 1999, p.124
6. DesAutels et al., Larry May, 'Challenging Medical Authority', p.72
7. Hitchcock, Vol II, p.126
8. This is a theme of my *Morality Matters*, Blackwell, Oxford, 2005
9. Paton Yoder, 'The Amish View of the State' in *The Amish and the State*, ed. Donald B. Kraybill (2nd edition) Johns Hopkins University Press, Baltimore, 2003, p.28
10. Kraybill, Lee Zook, 'Slow Moving Vehicles', p.156
11. Kraybill, p.160
12. Kraybill, Thomas J. Meyers, 'Education and Schooling', p.100
13. *Wisconsin v. Yoder* 406 U.S. 205 (1972)
14. 406 U.S. 234
15. See *The Economist*, February 7th 2004
16. See my *Morality Matters*, pp. 78–81
17. *Leyla Sahin v. Turkey*, (Grand Chamber) Application no 44774/98, 10th November 2005
18. *Leyla Sahin v. Turkey*, (Chamber) Application no. 44774/98, 29th June 2004, #27–9
19. *Leyla Sahin*, (Chamber) #36
20. *Leyla Sahin*, (Chamber) #Par 100
21. *R v. Headteacher and Governors of Denbigh High School* (2006) UKHL15
22. EWCt Civ 199, #73 (2005)
23. EWCt Civ 199 #76
24. UKHL 15, #34 (2006)
25. #93
26. #72

27. Marci A. Hamilton, *God vs. the Gavel: Religion and the Rule of Law*, Cambridge University Press, New York, 2005, p.275
28. Hamilton, p.304

CHAPTER 4

1. M. Scalabrino, (ed.) *International Code on Religious Freedom*, Peeters, Leuven, 2003, p.153
2. John Locke, *Political Essays*, ed. M. Goldie, Cambridge University Press, Cambridge, 1997, 'Essays on the Law of Nature', VI, p.117
3. Locke, 'An Essay on Toleration', p.137
4. Locke, p.138
5. Locke, p.138
6. Locke, p.157
7. Locke, p.159
8. See Locke's *The Reasonableness of Christianity*, Thoemmes Press, Bristol, 1997
9. Locke, p.138
10. See Jeremy Waldron, *God, Locke and Equality*, Cambridge University Press, Cambridge, 2002, ch. 8, particularly p.226
11. Locke, p.142
12. Locke, p.152
13. Locke, p.159
14. Locke, p.137
15. *Second Treatise*, ed. P. Laslett, Cambridge University Press, Cambridge, 1988, p.4
16. See Charles Taliaferro and Alison J. Teply (eds) *Cambridge Platonist Spirituality*, Paulist Press, New York, 2004
17. Waldron, p.2
18. Waldron, p.3
19. See my *Ideas of Human Nature*, 2nd edition, Blackwell, Oxford, 1999 ch.10

20. See my *Morality Matters*, Blackwell, Oxford, 2005, e.g. p.147
21. Robert J. Sharpe, Katherine E. Swinton, Kent Roach, *The Charter of Rights and Freedoms*, 2nd edition, Irwin Law, Toronto, 2002, p.324
22. Sharpe et al., p.328

CHAPTER 5

1. See my *Understanding Social Science*, 2nd edition, Blackwell, Oxford, 2000, particularly ch. 3
2. Bhikhu Parekh, *Rethinking Multiculturalism: Cultural Diversity and Political Theory*, Palgrave, London, 2000, p.146
3. Parekh, p.161
4. Parekh, p.162
5. K. A. Appiah, *The Ethics of Identity*, Princeton University Press, Princeton, NJ, 2005, p.78
6. Appiah, p.85
7. See M. Scalabrino (ed.), *International Code on Religious Freedom*, Peeters, Leuven, 2003, p.135
8. Abdullah Saheed and Hassan Saheed, *Freedom of Religion, Apostasy and Islam*, Ashgate, Aldershot, 2004, p.98.
9. M. H. Ogilvie, *Religious Institutions and the Law in Canada*, 2nd edition, Irwin Law, Toronto, 2003, p.60
10. Parekh, p.239
11. Parekh, p.240
12. See my *Reason and Commitment*, Cambridge University Press, Cambridge, 1973
13. Parekh, p.240
14. *Pretty v. United Kingdom*, 2346/02, 29th April 2002, #82
15. *Pichon and Sajous v. France*, EctHR 2nd October 2001
16. Scalabrino, p.153

17. J. Hitchcock, *The Supreme Court and Religion in American Life*, Vol II, Princeton University Press, Princeton, NJ, 2004, p.127
18. Pet Brief at 5
19. See website www.saint-hubert.org
20. *Cutler v. Wilkinson*, 125 S. Ct. 2113 2123 (2005)
21. *Cutler*, 125 S. Ct. at 2123
22. *Cutler*, 125 S. Ct. at 2124 n.13

Chapter 6

1. R. J. Sharpe et al. (eds), *The Charter of Rights and Freedoms*, 2nd edition, Irwin Law, Toronto, 2002, p.321
2. J. Rawls, *The Law of Peoples*, Harvard University Press, Cambridge, MA, 1999, p.127
3. Rawls, p.150
4. See my *Morality Matters*, Blackwell, Oxford, 2005, p.85ff
5. *Laïcité et Republique, Rapport au President de la Republique sur L'Application du Principe de Laïcité dans la Republique, Le 11 Decembre 2003 Remis au President de la Republique*, La Documentation Francaise, Paris, 2004, p.53
6. Guy Coq, *Laïcité et Republique*, Editions du Felin, Paris, 1995, p.17
7. See *Laïcité et Republique, Rapport de la Commission sur L'Application du Principe de Laïcité*
8. *Rapport de la Commission*, p.5
9. *Rapport*, p.45
10. *Rapport*, p.21
11. *Rapport*, p.40
12. *Rapport*, p.5
13. *Rapport*, p.130
14. *Rapport*, p.71
15. *Rapport*, p.73
16. Romans 13:1

17. *Rapport*, p.35
18. *Rapport*, p.37
19. *Rapport*, p.38
20. Coq, p.28
21. Coq, p.93
22. *Rapport*, p.126
23. *Rapport*, p.126
24. J. S. Mill, 'On Liberty', p.200

CHAPTER 7

1. J. Habermas: 'Religious Toleration: The Pacemaker for Cultural Rights', *Philosophy*, 2004
2. See my *Rationality and Religion*, Blackwell, Oxford, 1998
3. See my *Reason and Commitment*, Cambridge University Press, Cambridge, 1973
4. Abdullah Saeed and Hassan Saeed, *Freedom of Religion, Apostasy and Islam*, Ashgate, Aldershot, 2004, p.19
5. Saeed and Saeed, p.16
6. Carolyn Evans, *Freedom of Religion under the European Convention of Human Rights*, Oxford University Press, Oxford, 2001, p.28
7. Evans, p.28
8. Evans, p.3
9. M. Walzer, *On Toleration*, Yale University Press, New Haven, CT, 1997, p.71
10. Walzer, p.70
11. See my *Morality Matters*, Blackwell, Oxford, 2005
12. *Metropolitan Church of Bessarabia v. Moldova*, E.Ct H.R. 13th December 2001, (Application no. 45701/99) p.32
13. *Bessarabia v. Moldova*, p.32
14. *Bessarabia v. Moldova*, p.28
15. *Bessarabia v. Moldova*, p.26

16. *Bessarabia v. Moldova*, p.27
17. M. Warnock (ed.), *Utilitarianism*, J. S. Mill. 'On Liberty', p.143, Fontana, London, 1962
18. Warnock, p.145
19. *Bessarabia v. Moldova*, p.27

CHAPTER 8

1. The Canadian Charter of Rights and Freedoms is reproduced in Robert J. Sharpe, Katherine E. Swinton, Kent Roach, *The Charter of Rights and Freedoms*, 2nd edition, Irwin Law, Toronto, 2002
2. See Kent Roach, *The Supreme Court on Trial: Judicial Activism or Democratic Dialogue*, Irwin Law, Toronto, 2001
3. *R. v. Big M Drug Mart*, (1985), Canadian Supreme Court, 1SCR 296
4. Peter W. Hays, 'Equality as a Charter Value' 2003, 20 Sup. Ct. L. Rev. (2d), p.118
5. Beverley McLauchin, 14 Sup. Ct. L. Rev (2d) 2001, p.21
6. *Copsey v. WWB Devon Clays Ltd* (2005) EWCA Civ 932 #31
7. EWCA Civ 932 #38
8. *R. v. Big M Drug Mart*, p.347
9. *R. v. Big M Drug Mart*, p.351
10. David M. Brown 'Freedom From or Freedom For', 33 UBCCR 551 2000
11. Brown, p.305
12. M. H. Ogilvie, 'The Unbearable Lightness of Charter Canada', *Journal of Church Law*, 3, 2002, p.207
13. *Bal v. Ontario* (1994) 21 O.R. 3d 682
14. Bruce MacDougall 'The Separation of Church and Date' *UBC Law Review*, 36, 2003, p.12
15. MacDougall, p.22
16. Section 58 2004 SCC 79, *Reference re Same-Sex Marriage*,
17. *Reference*, Section 21
18. *Reference*, Section 22

19. *Reference*, Section 23
20. *Reference*, Section 27
21. See my *Morality Matters*, chapters 1 and 2 for a discussion of human flourishing and what is 'natural'

CHAPTER 9

1. Paul Hirst, 'Morals, Religion and the Maintained School', *British Journal of Educational Studies*, 4, 1965, p.11
2. Hirst, p.12
3. Robert Jackson, *Rethinking Religious Education and Plurality*, Routledge Falmer, London, 2004, p.36
4. Jackson, p.57
5. Jackson, p.145
6. Clive Ericker and Jane Ericker, *Reconstructing Religious, Spiritual and Moral Education*, RoutledgeFalmer, London, 2000, p.59
7. Ericker and Ericker, p.76
8. *Laïcité et Republique, Rapport au President de la Republique*, La Documentation Francaise, Paris, p.137
9. *The Secretary's Statement on Religious Expression*, U.S. Department of Education (www.ed.gov/Speeches/08-1995/religion)
10. See my *Ideas of Human Nature*, Blackwell, Oxford, 2nd edition, 1999
11. Kent Greenawalt, *Does God Belong in Public Schools?* Princeton University Press, Princeton, NJ, 2005, p.67
12. Greenawalt, p.153
13. Greenawalt, p.133
14. Greenawalt, p.137
15. Jackson, p.166
16. Section 8:3
17. *Religious Education: The Non-Statutory National Framework*, Qualifications and Curriculum Authority, London, 2004, p.3

18. *Framework*, p.8
19. *Framework*, p.11
20. *Framework*, p.13
21. Speech by H.M. The Queen at the Opening of the 8th General Synod of the Church of England, 15th November 2005 (www.royal.gov.uk)
22. *Framework*, p.13
23. B. V. Hill, *Exploring Religion in Schools: A National Priority*, Openbook, Adelaide, 2004, p.77
24. Hill, p.136
25. Hill, p.178
26. Hill, p.186
27. Hill, p.196
28. See my *Rationality and Religion*, Blackwell, Oxford, 1998
29. Hill, p.164

CHAPTER 10

1. Gianni Vattimo, *Nihilism and Emancipation*, Columbia University Press, New York, 2004, p.47
2. Vattimo, p.56
3. R. Rorty, *Philosophy and Social Hope*, Penguin, Harmondsworth, 1999, p.xxv
4. Rorty, p.169
5. Richard Rorty and Gianni Vattimo, *The Future of Religion*, Columbia University Press, New York, 2005, p.36
6. J. Rawls, *Political Liberalism*, Columbia University Press, New York, 1993, p.xix
7. Rawls, p.67
8. Rawls, p.67
9. *The Federalist Papers*, No 10, Signet Classics, New York, 2003, p.73

Chapter 11

1. *Elk Grove v. Newdow*, 124 S.Ct. 2301, 2318 (2004) (Rehnquist, C.J., concurring)
2. J. Hitchcock, *The Supreme Court and Religion in American Life*, Princeton University Press, Princeton, NJ, 2004, Vol II, p.26
3. Hitchcock, Vol II, p.30
4. See Philip Hamburger, *Separation of Church and State*, Harvard University Press Cambridge, MA, 2002
5. *The Federalist Papers*, No 51, Signet Classics, New York, 2003, p.320
6. *Federalist Papers*, p.321
7. See Hamburger, p.104
8. *Elk Grove*, 124 S.Ct. at 2331 (Thomas, J., concurring)
9. *Lemon v. Kurtzman*, 403, U.S. 602, 612–13 (1971)
10. *Zelman v. Simmons-Harris*, 536 U.S. 639 (2002)
11. *Locke v. Davey*, 124 S.Ct. 1307 (2004)
12. *Locke*, 124 S.Ct. at 1308
13. *Locke*, 124 S.Ct. at 1311
14. *Locke*, 124 S.Ct. at 1316 (Scalia, J., dissenting)
15. *Locke*, 124 S.Ct. at 1320 (Scalia, J., dissenting)
16. *Locke*, 124 S.Ct. at 1316 (Scalia, J., dissenting)
17. *Elk Grove*, 124 S.Ct. at 2306
18. *Elk Grove*, 124 S.Ct. at 2306–07
19. *Lee v. Weisman*, 505 U.S. 577 (1992)
20. *Elk Grove*, 124 S.Ct. at 2321 (O'Connor, J., concurring)
21. *Elk Grove*, at 2321
22. *Elk Grove*, at 2322
23. *Elk Grove*, at 2322
24. *Elk Grove*, at 2326
25. *Elk Grove*, at 2325
26. *Elk Grove*, 124 S.Ct. at 2319 (Rehnquist, C.J., concurring)
27. *Gonzales v. O Centro Espirita Benficente Uniao Do Vegetal*, 126 S.Ct. 1211, 1217 (2006)

28. *Gonzales,* 126 S.Ct. at 1216
29. Hitchcock, Vol II, p.144
30. Hitchcock, Vol II, p.60
31. *Elk Grove,* 124 S.Ct. at 2331 (Thomas, J., concurring)
32. Hitchcock, Vol II, p.112
33. *ACLU Nebraska Foundation v. Plattsmouth,* 358 F. 3d 1020, 1026 (8th Cir. 2004)
34. *ACLU Nebraska Foundation,* 358 F. 3d at 1036
35. *ACLU Nebraska Foundation,* 358 F. 3d at 1038
36. *ACLU Nebraska Foundation v. Plattsmouth,* 419 F. 3d 772, 778 (8th Cir. 2005)
37. *ACLU Nebraska Foundation,* 419, F. 3d at 781 (Bye, J., dissenting)
38. *Van Orden v. Perry,* 125 S.Ct. 2854, 2859 (2005)
39. *Van Orden,* 125 S.Ct. at 2861
40. *McCreary County, Kentucky v. American Civil Liberties Union of Kentucky,* 125 S.Ct. 2722, 2751 (Scalia, J., dissenting) (2005)
41. *McCreary,* 125 S.Ct. at 2733
42. *McCreary,* 125 S.Ct. at 2747 (O'Connor, J., concurring)
43. De Tocqueville A., *Democracy in America,* Vol I, Everyman, p.306
44. *McCreary,* 125 S.Ct. at 2733 n.10

Conclusion

1. *Van Orden v. Perry,* 125 S.Ct. 2854, 2890 (2005) (Stevens, J., dissenting)
2. *Van Orden,* 125, S.Ct. at 2889 (Stevens, J., dissenting)
3. *Van Orden,* 125, S.Ct. at 2890 (Stevens, J., dissenting)

Bibliography

ACLU Nebraska Foundation, John Doe v. City of Plattsmouth, U.S. Court of Appeals for 8th Circuit, 02-2444, 2004

APPIAH, K. A. *The Ethics of Identity*, Princeton University Press, Princeton, NJ, 2005

AUDI, R. *Religious Commitment and Secular Reason*, Cambridge University Press, Cambridge, 2000

Bal v. Ontario (1994) 21. OR 3d

BROWN, D. M. 'Freedom From or Freedom For', 33 UBCCR 2000

Copsey v. WWB Devon Clays Ltd (2005) EWCA civ 932

COQ, GUY, *Laïcité et Republique: Le Lien Nécessaire*, Editions du Felin, Paris, 1995

Cutter v. Wilkinson, 544 US 2005

DESAUTELS, P., BATTIN, M. P., and MAY, L. *Praying for a Cure*, Rowman and Littlefield, Lanham, MD, 1999

Elk Grove v. Newdow, 503 US 2004

ERICKER, C., and ERICKER, J. *Reconstructing Religious, Spiritual and Moral Education*, RoutledgeFalmer, London, 2000

EVANS, C. *Freedom of Religion under the European Convention of Human Rights*, Oxford University Press, Oxford, 2001

FERGUSON, D. *Church, State and Civil Society*, Cambridge University Press, Cambridge, 2004

FERRARI, S., and DURHAM, W. C., Jr. (eds) *Law and Religion in Post-Communist Europe*, Peeters, Leuven, 2003

Bibliography

Gonzales v. O Centro Espirita Beneficente Uniao Do Vegetal, 546 US (2006)

GREENAWALT, K. *Does God Belong in Public Schools?* Princeton University Press, Princeton, NJ, 2005

HABERMAS, J. *Religion and Rationality*, Polity Press, Cambridge, 2002

—— 'Religious Toleration: The Pacemaker for Cultural Rights', *Philosophy*, 79, 2004

HAMBURGER, P. *Separation of Church and State*, Harvard University Press, Cambridge, MA, 2002

HAMILTON, A., MADISON, J., JAY, J. *The Federalist Papers*, ed. C. Rossiter, Signet Classic, New York, 2003

HAYS, P. W. 'Equality as a Charter Value', 20 Sup. Ct. L.Rev. (2d) Ottawa, 2003

HILL, B. V. *Exploring Religion in Schools: a National Priority*, Openbook, Adelaide, 2004

HIRST, P. 'Morals, Religion and the Maintained School', *British Journal of Educational Studies*, 4, 1965

HITCHCOCK, J. *The Supreme Court and Religion in American Life*, Vol I: *The Odyssey of the Religion Clauses*; Vol II: *From 'Higher Law' to 'Sectarian Scruples'* Princeton University Press, Princeton, NJ, 2004

JACKSON, R. *Rethinking Religious Education and Plurality*, Routledge-Falmer, London, 2004

KRAYBILL, D. B. (ed.) *The Amish and the State*, Johns Hopkins University Press, Baltimore, MD, 2nd edition, 2003

Laïcité et Republique, Rapport de la Commission sur L'Application du Principe de Laïcité dans la Republique, Paris, La Documentation Francaise, 2004

Lee v. Weisman, 503 US 1992

Leyla Sahin v. Turkey, EctHR 44774/98, 29th June 2004

LOCKE, J. *Two Treatises of Government*, ed. P. Laslett, Cambridge University Press, Cambridge, 1988

—— *Political Essays*, ed. Mark Goldie, Cambridge University Press, Cambridge, 1997

Bibliography

LOCKE, J. *The Reasonableness of Christianity*, Thoemmes Press, Bristol, reprint of 1794 edition, 1997

MACDOUGALL, B. 'The Separation of Church and Date: Destabilizing Traditional Religion-Based Legal Norms on sexuality', *UBC Law Review* 36, 2003

MCLAUCHIN, B. 14 Sup. Ct. L.Rev. (2d) Ottawa, 2001

McCreary County, Kentucky v. ACLU, Kentucky, 545 US 2005

Metropolitan Church of Bessarabia v. Moldova, E.Ct.H.R. Application no 45701/99, 13th December 2001

MILL, J. S. 'On Liberty', *Utilitarianism*, ed. Mary Warnock, Fontana, London, 1962

OGILVIE, M. H. 'The Unbearable Lightness of Charter Canada, *Journal of Church Law*, 3, 2002

—— *Religious Institutions and the Law in Canada*, Irwin Law, Toronto, 2nd edition, 2003

Organization for Security and Co-operation in Europe (OSCE), *Guidelines for Review of Legislation Pertaining to Religion or Belief,* adopted by Venice Commission, and welcomed by OSCE Parliamentary Assembly, Edinburgh, 2004

PAREKH, BHIKHU, *Rethinking Multiculturalism: Cultural Diversity and Political Theory,* Palgrave, London, 2000

PICHON and SAJOUS v. France, E.Ct.H.R. 2nd October 2001

Pretty v. United Kingdom, E.Ct.H.R. 2346/02, 29th April 2002

R. v. Big M Drug Mart, Canadian Supreme Court (1985)1SCR 296

RAWLS, J. *Political Liberalism*, Columbia University Press, New York, 1993

—— *The Law of Peoples*, Harvard University Press, Cambridge, MA, 1999

Religious Education: The Non-Statutory National Framework, London, Qualifications and Curriculum Authority, 2004

Reference re Same Sex Marriage, 2004 SCC 79

Remmers v. Brewer 494 F.2d , U.S. 8th Circuit, 1974

ROACH, K. *The Supreme Court on Trial: Judicial Activism or Democratic Dialogue*, Irwin Law, Toronto, 2002

Bibliography

RORTY, R. *Philosophy and Social Hope*, Penguin, Harmondsworth, 1999

—— and VATTIMO, G. *The Future of Religion*, Columbia University Press, New York, 2005

SAHEED, A., and SAHEED H. *Freedom of Religion, Apostasy and Islam*, Ashgate, Aldershot, 2004

SCALABRINO, M. (ed.) *International Code on Religious Freedom*, Peeters, Leuven, 2003

Select Committee on Religious Offences in England and Wales, Volume 1–Report, House of Lords, London, 2002–3

SHARPE, R. J., SWINTON, K. E., and ROACH, K. *The Charter of Rights and Freedoms*, Irwin Law, Toronto, 2nd edition, 2002

TALIAFERRO, C., and TEPLY, A. J. (ed.) *Cambridge Platonist Spirituality*, Paulist Press, New York, NY, 2004

TAYLOR, C. *Modern Social Imageries*, Duke University Press, Durham, NC, 2004

THIESSEN, E. J. *In Defence of Religious Schools and Colleges*, McGill-Queen's University Press, Montreal, Quebec, and Kingston, Ontario, 2001

TRIGG, R. *Reason and Commitment*, Cambridge University Press, Cambridge, 1973

—— *Rationality and Science*, Blackwell, Oxford, 1993

—— *Rationality and Religion*, Blackwell, Oxford, 1998

—— *Ideas of Human Nature*, Blackwell, Oxford, 2nd edition, 1999

—— *Understanding Social Science*, Blackwell, Oxford, 2nd edition, 2000

—— *Morality Matters*, Blackwell, Oxford, 2005

United Kingdom Parliament: *Racial and Religious Hatred Bill, Explanatory Notes*, London: Session 2005–6

VATTIMO, G. *Nihilism and Emancipation*, Columbia University Press, New York, NY, 2004

Van Orden v. Perry, 545 US 2005

Bibliography

WALDRON, J. *God, Locke and Equality*, Cambridge University Press, Cambridge, 2002

WALZER, M. *On Toleration*, Yale University Press, New Haven, CT, 1997.

Wisconsin v. Yoder 406 US 1972

Index

255

Index

Index

Index

Index

Index